Emotional intelligence

An effective guide to master emotions, stop overthinking, enhance your EQ and improve social skills to become successful in life.

By

Damon Colmain

The trademarks that are used are without any consent, and the publication of the trademark is without permission or backing by the trademark owner. All trademarks and brands within this book are for clarifying purposes only and are owned by the owners themselves, not affiliated with this document.

Table Of Contents

Introduction

Peter Salovey and John D. Mayer coined the term ' Emotional Intelligence' in 1990. Daniel Goleman was aware of Salovey's work in the 1990s and Mayer. Goleman was a New York Times science writer specializing in brain and behavioral studies. He studied at Harvard as a psychologist, where he collaborated with David McClelland. McClelland was among an increasing group of researchers who became concerned about how little conventional cognitive intelligence tests were telling us what it takes to be successful in life.

Goleman concluded that what guaranteed business success was not logical intelligence but emotional intelligence. He defined emotionally intelligent people as those with four characteristics:

- They were good at recognizing their own emotions (soul-awareness)
- They were good at handling their emotions (self-management)
- They were empathetic to other people's emotional needs (social awareness)
- They were good at handling the emotions of other people (social skills)

Developing your EQ skills in a competitive workplace is key to your professional success. Use an assertive communication style to develop your emotional intelligence instead of responding to confrontation. Use active listening skills. Stay motivated. Find strategies to sustain a positive attitude. Empathize with others. Be sociable and open.

Demonstrate Good Interpersonal Communication. Teach them to recognize Subtle Differences and Dynamic Relationships among Emotions. Teach them to seek others ' support

Emotional intelligence helps people to improve their personal and professional relationships and increases our social skills.

Overthinking is something that wastes your resources, disables your decision-making ability, and keeps putting you on a loop of thought and worrying.

This is sort of thought that is wasting your time and resources and stopping you from doing, doing different things to make progress in your life.

Since we are all accountable and want to be devoted to our personal or professional life, it is our responsibility to be sufficient to our emotions, and to have a better emotional quotient could be a game-changer in your life.

Chapter 1: Introduction to Emotional Intelligence

For most people, emotional intelligence is essential to attaining success in their lives and careers than one's intellect (IQ). As an individual, our success and the success of the profession today depends on our ability to read and respond appropriately to the signals of other people.

Each of us, therefore, needs to develop the mature emotional intelligence skills needed to better understand, empathize, and negotiate with others— especially as the economy has become more global. Otherwise, success in our lives and careers will evade us.

"The EQ is the extent of your ability to understand other people, what motivates them, and how to work with them in collaboration," says Howard Gardner, the prominent theorist at Harvard.

1.1 What Are Emotions?

Emotions seem to control our everyday lives. Whether we're happy, angry, sad, bored, or frustrated, we make decisions. We select activities and hobbies based on the emotions that they prompt.

Defining Emotions

An emotion is a complex psychological state involving three distinct components:

- A subjective experience,
- A physiological response, and
- A behavioral or expressive response.

In addition to attempting to define what the emotions are, researchers have also attempted to identify and classify the types of emotions. The descriptions have changed over time:

1. In 1972, psychologist Paul suggested that there are six basic emotions throughout human cultures: fear, disgust, anger, surprise, happiness, and sadness.

2. In 1999, he extended this list to add a number of other basic emotions, including embarrassment, excitement, contempt, shame, pride, satisfaction, and amusers.

Robert Plutchik created another emotional classification system known as the "wheel of emotions" in the 1980s. This model demonstrated how various emotions could be blended or mixed together, much the way an artist combines primary colors to produce other colors.

3 Plutchik suggested eight primary emotional dimensions:

- Joy vs. sorrow,
- Indignation vs. fear,
- Trust vs. disgust, and
- Excitement vs. anticipation.

Then these feelings can be combined to create others (like joy + excitement= excitation).

Let us take three key elements, known as the subjective experience, the physiological response, and the behavioral response, to better understand what emotions are (Cherry, 2019).

1. The Subjective Experience

While experts believe that there are a variety of basic universal emotions that people around the world experience regardless of context or culture, researchers also claim that feeling emotions can be highly subjective. As we have broad labels for emotions such as "angry," sad, or "happy," your own experience of these emotions may be much more subjective

Take anger, for instance. Is all anger the same? Your own experience could be ranging from mild annoyance to blinding anger.

Plus, we don't always experience every emotion in pure forms. Mixed emotions are normal over various events or circumstances in our lives. You could feel both excited and nervous when faced with starting a new job.

Marrying or raising a child could be characterized by a wide range of emotions ranging from happiness to anxiety. These emotions could happen at the same time, or you might feel them one after another.

2. The psychological response

If you have ever felt your stomach lurch from anxiety or your heart palpating with fear, then you know that feelings can cause intense physiological reactions. Or, as in the Cannon theory of emotion, we feel emotions and experience simultaneous physiological reactions.) Many of the physiological reactions you experience during an emotion, such as sweaty hands or racing heartbeat, are controlled by the sympathetic nervous system, a division of the autonomic nervous system.

The autonomic nervous system controls body responses involuntarily, such as blood flow and digestion. The sympathetic nervous system is controlling the fight-or-flight responses in the body. Those responses will automatically prepare your body to flee from danger or face the threat head-on when faced with a threat.

Although early studies of emotional physiology tended to focus on those autonomous responses, more recent research has concentrated on the role of the brain in emotions. The amygdala, portion of the limbic system, plays a major role in emotion and fear in particular. The amygdala is a tiny structure linked to motivational states such as hunger and thirst, memory, and emotion.

Researchers have been using brain imaging to show that the amygdala becomes activated when people are shown threatening images. Damage to the amygdala has also proven to inhibit the response to fear.

3. The Behavioral Response

Perhaps the final part you're most familiar with — the actual expression of emotion. We spend considerable time decoding the emotional expressions of the people around us. Our ability to understand these expressions correctly is related to what psychologists call emotional intelligence, EI, and these expressions play a significant part in our body language as a whole.

Research suggests that many expressions, such as a smile to indicate happiness or a frown to indicate sadness, are universal. Sociocultural norms also play a part in the way emotions are expressed and interpreted.

In Japan, for example, when an authority figure is present, people tend to mask displays of fear or disgust. Likewise, Western cultures such as the United States are more likely to express negative emotions both on their own and in the presence of others, whereas eastern cultures such as Japan are more likely to do so alone.

We often use the words "emotions" and "moods" interchangeably in everyday language, but researchers often differentiate between the two actually. How are they different? An emotion is usually fairly short-lived, but intense. It is also likely that emotions will have a clear and observable resource.

For example, you may feel angry for a short period of time after you disagree with a friend about politics.

A mood, on the other hand, is typically much milder than an emotion, but longer-lasting.

In many situations, the specific cause of a mood can be difficult to identify. You may find yourself feeling depressed for several days, for example, without any simple, recognizable cause.

1.2How Our Lives are Affected by Emotions?

Memory

Our experiences are very closely tied to our emotions. The more emotional something is usually to us, the more unforgettable it will be. If an incident in our life causes us to experience extreme emotion, we are more likely to remember the event.

For example, certain emotional family holiday events may cause you to have strong vacation memories.

Such memories will leave you feeling good or bad about the holidays. You may have a great holiday memory because you first had to see the ocean, and you absolutely loved it. If you were badly sunburned on the first day at the beach, though, you might have a bad memory of that holiday. Or if you were either trapped in an undertaking or stung by a jellyfish, this terrifying recollection may cause you to feel negative about the ocean or even family holidays in general.

2. Decision making

Such emotional memories are very important to help us make decisions in the future. Following the example of the family holiday above, if we have a good holiday experience, if we are faced with next year's decision to leave with the kids, you're likely to decide to leave again. But if your holiday memory wasn't that great, it will also influence how you decide on future family holidays. If you recall how you felt sunburned on the first day of your holiday, you might think of several options:

a) Go somewhere you're not going to be on a beach,

b) Bring better sun protection or

c) Don't go

A similar process of thinking will take place if you remember the feeling you felt when you were trapped in an ocean undertow. You may:

a) Go somewhere where there is no ocean

b) Learn to be more cautious or decide not to go into the sea or

c) Decide not to go out.

It becomes important to understand our emotions when weighing the options and ultimately making a decision. The better we understand our emotions (and from what this emotion derives), the better decisions we make.

We're learning from our memories. When our emotional memory of the sunburn is so high, it can cause us to have an overall negative relationship with the holiday, making you decide not to go on holiday next time. Ideally, that won't be the case because you've investigated where this negative emotion originated from and eventually decide that if you're more cautious in the sun, you might be able to go and have a great time possibly.

If you remember that your fear surrounding the holiday had to do with being careless in the water, it won't stop you from going on family holidays altogether. If we don't understand where feelings come from, we may make some bad or unreasonable decisions. Some of those options would be unreasonable if we add our emotions to the whole situation (vacation) for one case (sunburn). It wouldn't make sense to never go on holiday again because we equated the holiday with anger or fear when that fear and anger were the product of only one occurrence throughout the holiday.

We have to understand what caused the anger (due to sunburn not being able to be on the beach) or fear being caught. This understanding will be helpful for us to make better futures decisions.

3.Behavior

Our feelings guide us. It is what is driving us to act. It's what helped keep us alive in primitive times. Something to fear would trigger "battle" or "run."

We tackle it either head-on or run away. Once we developed and became more civilized, we had to act fast or die. Society gradually became more civilized, and our global success now demands that we consider before we act. As a result, our brains started to develop in ways that encouraged us to stop thinking about the consequences of our actions before acting instinctively on an emotion.

Act before we think: In this universe, there are inherent causes (typically threats) that will cause us to act before we think. Our brains are processing a threatening event, and we almost immediately respond.

Think before we act: Most situations don't require an instant response. We may want to hit something or someone if something makes us upset, but our brains require us to think through the consequences of this.

Hitting someone can temporarily cause us to feel good. But, in the long run, things like jail or being sued, or losing a best friend or loved one, will have consequences. The long-term consequences could make us feel much worse than the initial relief that could come from hitting someone.

Very often, we are responding to the behaviors of other people based on how we feel about ourselves.

If we are uncertain or unsure about ourselves, we are much more likely to have a negative emotional response to positive remarks or behavior from someone. For instance, if I think I'm fat, and my husband tells me, "Will you eat that?"I could assume he thought I shouldn't eat that because it's going to make me fatter. Result-I gets angry with him and shouts at him. This would be unfortunate as he most likely meant he wanted the last piece to be his own. If we stopped thinking about why somebody did or said something made us angry, we may be able to respond more appropriately. We shouldn't be punishing others for our own feelings.

Being more conscious of that can prevent us from acting inappropriately.

4. Relationships

Our relationships build on our ability to process and understand our and other emotions. We need to consider how the people we communicate with behave when communicating with others. If the individual is sad, then we should display the appropriate concern (that is, comfort them). If the individual is upset, we should want to figure out why and try to solve the problem (especially if it is us they are mad at). If we don't respond adequately to the emotions of others, it is assumed that we don't care. Typically this is not a desirable feature in anybody a friend, a partner, a family member, a manager, or an employee.

Our feelings: We have to express or pass on our emotions to others. If others can't read us, they won't know how to answer our needs. We must be honest with ourselves when understanding our emotions and be direct when communicating them to others.

It would appear that most miscommunicated emotions are sadness and fear. This is not a scientific finding; it is merely a general comment. So often, when we are feeling another emotion, primarily sad or fearful, we wrongly express anger. It's not always a conscious thing, but a vulnerability reaction that we might not be aware of unless we think about what we feel and why.

Miss-communicating Sad:

If we feel sad, then we have to convey that to others. So often, when we feel sad, we don't transmit that information properly. We put on a first act tough and show anger for whatever reason when we are really hurting.

Someone might hurt us, and we might be mad. But if anyone hurts us, we should be wary of showing (or expressing) sadness and not anger.

People usually hurt us unintentionally, and just need to be told why they hurt us.

Miss-communicating Fear or anxiety:

People with brain injury often face varying cognitive impairments. As they get to know these impairments, they get afraid not to return to who they were and the possibility that they will never function normally again. If someone asks why they can't find something of theirs, blow-up would be a typical reaction. Instantly they become defensive.

To them, it is a reminder of how their lives have changed. Now someone is confronting them with it and waiting for a reply. They don't want to face the reality of their brain injury, so it gets turned around-"What's the big deal? Why are you always picking on me? Leave me alone (cmf, 2012).

1.3 Defining Emotional Intelligence

A lot of us know about the IQ (Intelligence Quotient). This generates a score from a series of tests designed to measure intellectual intelligence. Higher IQs reflect greater cognitive abilities, or the ability to understand and know. Individuals with high IQs are more likely to do academically well without having to exert an equal amount of mental effort as those with low IQ scores.

Therefore a logical assumption is that people with higher IQs will be more successful at work and throughout their lives. This theory has proved to be wrong–there's more to success than just being' clever.'

Emotional Intelligence (EI or sometimes EQ-Emotional Quotient) is a more modern concept and was created by Daniel Goleman in the mid-1990s, among others.

Definition:

Emotional intelligence refers to a person's ability to regulate and control his or her emotions and also to have the ability to control others' emotions. We can also affect other people's emotions, in other words. Did you ever look back on some of the major decisions you made in your life and wonder, "What you were thinking? "And "why did you do that? "It may be to blame for those poor decisions and actions you have not used your emotional intelligence (EI).

Emotional Intelligence (EQ) is the capability to effectively and positively identify, utilize, understand, and manage emotions. A high EQ helps people communicate better, minimize anxiety and stress, defuse conflicts, strengthen relationships, empathize with others, and successfully overcome the challenges of life.

The quality of our lives is influenced by our emotional intelligence because it affects our actions. EQ is synonymous with self-awareness because it helps us to live our lives with meaning, intent, and autonomy.

Based on our current situations, many of us travel through life, making important decisions. We may view them as beyond our ability to change and therefore restrict our options and solutions. Having time to reflect on and evaluate why we want to do what we do allows us to lead lives decided by our deliberate decisions rather than just circumstances.

The performance may be greatly influenced by increasing EQ. Our personal situations and knowledge are also factors; however, EQ may have a profound effect on our decisions by generating opportunities that we may not otherwise have seen or viewed as possibilities.

Here are some examples of actions that exhibit emotional intelligence:

An emotionally intelligent athlete can acknowledge his loss when losing a match and encourage himself to feel sad about it, but he won't dwell on the disappointment. In analyzing what he did wrong, he will see it as an opportunity to improve.

When an employee regularly commits errors at work, and the emotionally intelligent boss will not automatically reprimand the employee or even ask why he repeatedly makes the same mistakes. The manager is conscious that asking the employee why questions could make the person feel ashamed and inferior. The boss then demonstrates empathy by thinking about how the person feels about the effects of his job. The purpose here is always to correct the conduct rather than to judge the individual.

When, in a given situation, whether at work or in personal life, he does not get what he wants, an emotionally intelligent person will not play the victim or blame others. He will understand feelings of anger or disappointment but will maintain self-control and communicate it in a healthy manner. They won't actively or deliberately show these negative emotions, but will recognize those emotions and look at the facts that caused him to be upset in an objective way.

1.4 Why Emotional Intelligence matters?

EQ is not IQ's enemy. High levels of both can be had. Life is, however, an inherently sociable construct. Without the ability to function well in this sense of relationships, it is unclear how far knowledge alone will get you. As Theodore Roosevelt put it: "No one knows how much you know unless they know how much you care." EQ is the nature of being human in many respects.

Emotional intelligence, and our capability to draw on it as a reserve, support us in so many ways: from caring for our physical and mental health and well-being to encouraging and leading ability. It's there when it comes to conflict resolution in our ability to manage successful partnerships and our armor and shield. It is the engine of growth in so many different ways.

EQ, as a quality catalyst, does not refer only to our personal lives. It also applies to the workplace. People with average IQ's score 70 percent of the time over those with the highest IQs. Is EQ the cause? Although EQ and IQ aren't rivals. Is emotional quotient a better indicator of success? Given that, according to the Center for Creative Leadership, 75 percent of careers are "derailed for reasons related to emotional skills, including the inability to handle interpersonal problems; unsatisfactory team leadership in difficult times or conflict; or inability to adapt to change or build confidence," it may be.

Importance of emotional intelligence

The word 'Emotional Intelligence,' first coined by psychologists Mayer and Salovey (1990), refers to one's ability to accurately and effectively interpret, process, and control emotional information, both within oneself and in others, and to use this knowledge to direct one's thoughts and actions and to influence others'.

Emotional intelligence may lead us on the road to a fulfilled and happy life by providing a structure for applying intelligence principles to emotional responses, and recognizing that these responses may be logically consistent or incompatible with particular emotional beliefs.

As the workplace changes, so do the research body supporting that individuals (from interns to managers) with higher EI are better equipped to function cohesively within teams, cope more effectively with change, and manage stress–thereby allowing them to achieve business goals more efficiently.

Goleman (1995) recognized five distinct categories of skills that are the key features of EI and suggested that, unlike the intelligence quotient (IQ), these categorical skills can be learned where they are absent and improved where they are present.

Therefore, EI, unlike its relatively fixed counterpart, IQ, is instead a complex component of one's personality and contains behavioral traits that can produce significant benefits when worked on, ranging from personal happiness and well-being to elevated professional success (Houston, 2020).

Chapter 2: Power of emotional intelligence

2.1 Power of emotional intelligence in the digital age

Human emotions and the market environment tend to be different and distinct environments. It may be, but when it comes to business, people always get involved, and emotions come with people.

We all know that if we wish to learn quickly, apply that knowledge, and use sound reasoning, having a good level of intelligence (IQ) is important. But we cannot oppose that human emotion is also a driving force in business today, particularly now when technology is advancing to the point where it is possible to automate many routine jobs.

As humans, we all have different emotional approaches and levels. Some are much more "in control" while others are energized to remain optimistic and make timely decisions. We all show different types of emotions depending on the people and circumstances around us, and we must have a high level of emotional intelligence, or EQ, to be able to control this.

The dictionary defines emotional intelligence as "the ability to understand and use this ability to make good decisions and to prevent or solve problems." Now you understand why all of us in the business world need this attribute, and even more so.

Look around to our world today to clearly understand emotional intelligence and its strength. When technology advances, we see a change in activities such as data entry, customer service, email marketing, and so on, becoming automated.

The machines performing these tasks are more accurate than humans, but a lot of things they can't do still. It is here that human emotion and emotional intelligence enter.

Machines can not yet fully replicate human emotion or the ability to understand and respond to it. Here are some forms in this digital age where emotional intelligence becomes a powerful ability.

First, critical analysis and decision-making require emotional intelligence. Machines are able to perform several tasks as long as they are trained to perform certain tasks. Yet machines can't always solve complex problems or make their own decisions.

The reason emotional intelligence is needed when solving complex problems and making tough decisions is that it involves human emotions. If we are trying to solve a problem that is highly customer-specific, you'll need emotional intelligence.

Second, deeper understanding includes emotional intelligence— something that computers still don't have. Deeper understanding encompasses both one's attitude and empathy towards others. To put ourselves in other's shoes, we need openness to listen and empathy.

In a world where everything can be automated, the human touch loses everything. Human emotion and deeper understanding are still required to create a great customer experience or to work truly in harmony with one another.

Third, your job or business life and your personal life need emotional intelligence. A machine— that is, your phone — can help you communicate with others, but it requires a sound level of emotional intelligence to be able to speak in some way. The second point in a way relates to social competences. Emotional intelligence is related to our ability to interact within our social environment. No matter how much technology advances, there is no running away from such issues as negotiation, conflict management, teamwork, and networking, all of which require emotional intelligence.

Last and possibly most importantly, emotional intelligence becomes crucial in a world where everything is accessible at our fingertips, where short attention spans, low patience, and reduced temper control prevail. We're all used to getting our way with a few clicks or taps and getting information. But many of the challenges that we face cannot be instantly clicked away. They still need time to understand and to solve.

This is emotional intelligence, which will help us to persevere over time. It allows us to better and healthily regulate our own emotions and control them. As we become aware of both our own emotions and those of others, we are in a position to react appropriately.

Emotional intelligence could be just one of the essential ingredients to keep you relevant. After all, these days, you need not only the technical skills to get the job done, but also the emotional intelligence to get it done more quickly and more effectively.

The good news is that one can learn and develop emotional intelligence. Nobody is born with the ability to understand their own emotions alongside those of others and react appropriately, but we can begin to develop this vital resource within ourselves by becoming self-aware (TALERNGSRI, 2019).

2.2 Benefits of Emotional Intelligence

You should simply ask yourself, "Do I have my feelings, or do they have me in a moment of positive or negative emotions? "Your emotional intelligence has an impact on a wide range of factors that contribute to individual and organizational success.

Here are ten benefits to becoming emotionally smarter:

1. Self-awareness —

People with high EQ are more understanding of themselves. They realize what they consider important and are committed to their own growth and development. They are open to feedback, which is going to help them improve. They are also highly sensitive to other people's feelings.

2. Communication —

Those with high emotional intelligence recognize the importance of clear and respectful communication. Faced with others' highly emotional reactions, they are able to remain calm. They know how to defuse defensiveness and find the underlying causes of an individual's emotional reactions. This allows them to influence others, more effectively solve the problems, and maintain the quality of their relationships.

3. Leadership —

Emotionally intelligent leaders are able to take positive control of themselves, their emotions, thoughts, and actions. Their self-control helps them behave consistently while influencing and connecting with the ones they manage. They build confidence and work towards maintaining a positive culture and conduct among their team members.

4. Change —

Implementing innovations and trying to adapt to the changes needed can become a source of frustration, anger, or a lack of empathy. People who are emotionally smart can manage the stress and anxiety often presented by the challenges of the change. Being able to handle a variety of tense situations helps to instill trust and trust in others while helping them to make progress in stressful times with greater ease and confidence.

5. Teamwork-

It's never easy to work with others and their different viewpoints.

Being able to share ideas openly and truly helps team members increase mutual respect while learning to appreciate differing points of view. Those who are emotionally intelligent don't manipulate or control the dynamics of the team to get what they want. Instead, they work together to provide approaches that are best for the business and the goals they seek to achieve.

6. Community —

Cultivating an atmosphere in which everyone values and supports one another creates a culture of mutual benefit and support. For those who work together, this sort of positive environment is fun and satisfying. Such a culture of teamwork improves productivity and creates goodwill among members of the company and teams.

7. Compassion —

Emotional intelligence fosters sympathy and compassion for others. Knowing how to approach and link with people helps understanding and respect building. It's key to being able to demonstrate empathy. Practicing empathy helps improving relationships, reduce stress and anxiety, and increase understanding at a time when meeting goals and deadlines are often more valued than humans.

8. Motivation —

Emotionally intelligent people are often optimistic and do not derail easily when faced with a challenge. They are hard workers with a mindset of growth and persevere in the time of difficulties. They are driven by a feeling of ambition to succeed no matter what the situation is and how infectious their energy is. When things get tough, they focus on purpose and process, rather than assigning blame to people and performance.

9. Productivity —

Because people with high emotional intelligence know how to handle conflict and contrasting beliefs effectively, they are not distracted by negative or "soft" emotions from others. During heated exchanges, they can manage themselves and know how to help others reclaim their rationality. Their skills help them to resolve problems more efficiently and handle conflicts. They are, therefore, more successful in their work activity and encourage others to do the same.

10. Relationships —

The nature of our relationships directly affects the esteem we have for each other, as well as the quality of the results we will achieve. One key to working effectively with others is knowing how to build and maintain effective relationships. People with high EQ do not personally take on other people's negative emotional reactions. Rather, they seek to understand the source of the feelings of others and the values that are important to others. It helps them to interact actively, rather than avoid those in the workplace who might respond more emotionally.

Those are a few of the benefits of becoming emotionally smarter. So what's the good news regarding EQ? The ability to become emotionally smarter can be learned and used to become more effective as an individual and as a leader. Your increased emotional quotient will not only help you manage your work and personal relationships but will also enhance your ability to more effectively lead and manage others (STOKER, 2018).

2.3 Emotional Intelligence Makes Creativity Happen

A new paper in the Creative Behavior Journal shows the power of emotional intelligence to bring about creativity.

The Faas Foundation collaborated on a survey of a representative sample of nearly 15,000 people across the United States and found that emotionally intelligent supervisors create

A climate that benefits creativity and innovation in those with whom they work.

What do smart, emotional supervisors do? First, they are able to read the feelings of workers, such as knowing when someone is frustrated or unhappy or concerned about changes at work. Not only can they read emotions, but they also explicitly acknowledge them.

Second, they help workers direct their emotions into important goals. They encourage passion and form decision making that takes into account both positive and negative voices (and historical issues and hopes).

Third, emotionally smart supervisors understand how different decisions or events affect workplace experiences. So eventually, when they are angry or irritated, they are able to manage their own feelings effectively, as well as support employees.

The Yale research, which was just released, asked three classes of questions. One set of questions asked humans to characterize the actions of their superiors. For example, how often does your boss know if someone is unhappy about a decision to take a job? How often does their supervisor get enthusiastic about motivating others?

Another set of questions asked about the emotional work experiences of people They asked them to describe how they typically feel in their own words about their work, and also asked them how often they face a long list of specific emotions, from feeling content, being respected and proud to feeling frustrated, angry or disheartened (and more!).

Finally, they asked how many opportunities they have to grow and make progress at work and how often they are creative at their work (e.g., contributing new ideas or original ways of achieving work goals).

The study shows that the work climate becomes more positive and supportive when supervisors acknowledge that employees have feelings and that these emotions matter. Employees described differing emotional experiences dramatically if they had managers who acted in emotionally intelligent ways or not. The quality of work relationships spilled into feelings about the duties and tasks of employees, and that, in turn, had an impact on creativity and innovation in what they had achieved. The study suggests that the emotional intelligence of supervisors is a job resource for their employees that helps both their well-being and successful work performance. When people were asked how they feel about work in their words, they say that work was linked with both positive and negative emotions. But two-thirds of the top feelings listed by those whose supervisors were emotionally smart were positive, while 70 percent of the top feelings mentioned by those whose supervisors were not emotionally smart were negative. Those whose supervisors were mentioned as emotionally intelligent were happier three times more often than stress. They mentioned growth-related feelings (e.g., being challenged, being fulfilled), feeling inspired, enjoying work, and feeling valued. Research in workplace psychology and organizational behavior shows that these feelings create the kind of environment conducive to optimal engagement and flourishing.

In comparison, those whose bosses most often do not show emotional intelligence report they were irritated and anxious. Such staffers reported being angry— they said they were frustrated, upset, annoyed, and crazy. On top of that, they also felt understated or totally unappreciated.

How do supervisors and leaders distinguish the ability of their employees to be creative? Organizational behavior scholars Jing Zhou and Jennifer George have demonstrated that emotionally smart supervisors know that emotions provide information about ourselves, the environment, and those around us. Employee dissatisfaction can be noticed by emotionally intelligent supervisors, who recognize that dissatisfaction conveys information about a real problem and can find a way to approach this problem as an opportunity for improvement. Emotionally smart bosses can control the feelings of their own and those of their employees to help with creative work. They can recognize when people are overly optimistic and can provide informative feedback preventing premature settling on ideas and inspiring persistence.

The Yale study shows that supervisors can create a climate where employees have opportunities to grow and where their jobs are inspired and motivated. Supervisors who recognize that employees are unable to leave emotions at the door, who recognize the feelings of employees, who understand where they come from and who help employees manage their feelings will have both happier and more creative staff. The results are relevant to anyone who influences others, such as teachers working with students or parents with their kids. The emotional climate that we create will affect both how those around us feel and what they can do (Pringle, 2020).

Chapter 3: Attributes of emotional intelligence

Emotional intelligence has the following attributes

- Self-awareness
- Empathy
- Motivation
- Self-regulation
- Social skills

3.1 Self-awareness

Simply put, self-awareness is consciousness, with the self-being that makes one's personality special. These unique components include ideas, experiences, and skills. More emotional intelligence in a person makes him more self-conscious.

The study of self-awareness in psychology can be traced back to 1972. The auto-consciousness theory was developed by psychologists Shelley Duval and Robert Wick Lund.

They proposed: "When we focus on ourselves, we assess and compare our current behavior with our internal standards and values. As objective evaluators of ourselves, we are self-conscious. "Ultimately, they consider self-consciousness a significant component of self-control.

Daniel Goleman proposed a definition of self-awareness as "knowing one's internal states, choices, resources, and intuitions." This definition places more emphasis on the capability to monitor our inner world, our thoughts and emotions as they arise.

It is important to know that self-awareness is not just about what we notice about ourselves, but also about how we notice our inner world and monitor it.

Have you ever held your own judgment regarding your thoughts or experiences? If yes, then you are not alone, and now is the time to work towards a self-reflection that is not judgmental.

This is more easily said than done, of course.

If non-judgmental consistency is an essential component of self-consciousness, how are we working towards it? As we notice what is going on inside of us, we can recognize and accept them as the inevitable part of being human, instead of giving ourselves a hard time.

If you ever said, "I should /shouldn't have done it" to yourself, then you know what it means. The next time you judge something you have said or done, consider the question: "Is what I've experienced an opportunity to learn and grow, too? Have other people made a similar mistake and learned from it? "Self-awareness goes beyond accumulating knowledge of ourselves: it is also about paying attention to our inner state, with the mind of a beginner and an open heart.

Our mind is extremely skilled at storing information about how we react to a particular event to form a blueprint for our emotional life. This knowledge also ends up shaping our minds to respond in some way as in the future; we experience a similar event.

Self-awareness helps us to be conscious of this mental conditioning and preconceptions, which can form the basis of liberating the mind from it.

Will Self-awareness Matter?

According to Daniel Goleman, self-awareness is the central pillar of emotional intelligence.

The capability to check our emotions and thoughts from moment to moment is essential to better understanding ourselves, being at peace with who we are, and controlling our thoughts, emotions, and behaviors proactively.

Additionally, people who are self-aware tend to act consciously (instead of reacting passively) and tend to be in good health and have a positive view on life. You also have a deeper experience of life and are more likely to have more compassion.

Sutton's investigation (2016) also looked at the component parts of self-awareness and its benefits.

This study found that self-reflection, insight, and awareness aspects of self-awareness can lead to benefits such as becoming a more accepting person, while aspects of rumination and awareness can lead to psychological burdens.

Different researches have shown self-awareness as a crucial feature of successful businessmen. In a study by Green Peak Partners and Cornell University, 72 executives were studied at both public and private firms. They all had profited from $50 million to $5 billion, and it has been found that "the strongest predictor of overall success was a high self-awareness score. Self-awareness — was the strongest predictor of overall success in this analysis.

Self-awareness is crucial for psychotherapists, too.

"Therapists need to know their own biases, values, stereotypical beliefs, and assumptions so as to serve culturally diverse clients appropriately" (Oden et al., 2009).

It was also called a "precursor to multicultural skills" (Buckley & Foldy, 2010). Self-awareness, in other words, allows counselors to understand the differences between their experiences and the experiences lived by their clients.

This can help counselors make their clients more non-judgmental and help them understand their clients better.

Why is Self-conscious Hard?

If self-consciousness is so important, why aren't we more self-aware?

The most obvious answer is that we're simply "not there" for observing ourselves most of the time. We are not there, in other words, to pay attention to what is going on inside or around us.

Psychologists Matthew Killings worth and Daniel T. Gilbert found that nearly half of the time, we're operating on "automatic pilot" or unconscious of what we're doing or how we're feeling, as our mind wanders to somewhere else than here and now.

Besides the constant wandering of mind, the different cognitive bias also affects our ability to have a precise understanding of ourselves; we tend to believe narratives that support our already existing sense of self.

For instance, if we have a strong belief that we are a high-quality and loyal friend, then we are likely to interpret events — even events where we may have made a mistake — as an anomaly of our identity as that "honest friend." This pre-existing belief in ourselves may affect how we handle the aftermath of, say, forgetting a lunch date with a friend.

In addition, confirmation bias may trick us into searching for or interpreting information in a manner that confirms our preconception of something .Have you ever had that feeling when you accepted a job offer but are still searching for extra assurance that this is the perfect job for you? That, in its finest, is confirmation bias.

In addition, the lack of willingness to receive input might also work against us if we want a more detailed view of ourselves through others' eyes.

If we wish to cultivate our own self-awareness, how do we reconcile that with these mental tendencies in which only certain versions of ourselves are recognized?

It's not easy, but some options do exist. What further complicates the picture is the various aspects of the self to which we contribute in everyday life.

Daniel Kahneman, for his contribution to behavioral science, is Nobel Prize winner.

Kahneman discusses the distinction between the "experiencing self" and the "remembering self" and how that influences our decision-making. He explains how we feel at the moment about the experience and how we remember the experience can be very different and share a correlation of only 50 percent.

This difference can have a major impact on the story we tell ourselves, the way we relate to ourselves and others, and the decision we make, even though most of the time, we might not notice the difference.

Cultivating Self-Awareness

Ways create some space for yourself. It is difficult to see things clearly when you are in a dark room without windows. The space you create is that crack on the wall where you allow light to pass through. Stay away from digital distractions and spend some time with yourself, reading, writing, meditating, and communicating with yourself–maybe first thing in the morning or half an hour before sleep.

Practice mindfulness

Mindfulness is the secret to self-confidence. Jon Kabat-Zinn defines awareness as "to pay attention in a particular way, purposefully, in the present moment, without judgment." By practicing awareness, you will be more with yourself, so that you can "be there" to realize what is going on in and around you. It is not about sitting with your legs crossed or suppressing your thoughts. It's about keeping an eye on your inner state as it emerges. You can exercise mindfulness whenever you want by listening carefully, eating, or walking.

Keep a journal

Writing not only helps us to process our thoughts but also makes us feel connected with ourselves and at peace. Writing will generate more headspace as well as letting your thoughts spill out to paper. Research shows that writing down things we're grateful for or even things we're struggling with helps increase happiness and contentment. You can use the journal to record your internal state, too. Try this at home–choose a half-day on the weekend, pay close attention to your inner world–what you feel, what you tell yourself, and take note of what you watch every hour. You might be surprised to hear what you write!

Practice being a good listener

Listening is not quite the same as hearing. Listening is about being present, paying full attention to the emotions, body movement, and language of other people. It is to show empathy and understand without evaluating or judging constantly. You'll also be better at listening to your own inner voice when you become a good listener and becoming your own best friend.

Ask for feedback

Sometimes we may be too scared to ask what others think of us— yes, sometimes the comments may be biased or even dishonest, but as you learn more about yourself and others, you will be capable of differentiating them from real and genuine feedback. Research has shown that conducting 360-degree feedback in the workplace is a useful tool for improving self-consciousness (Source) of managers (Jessie Zhu, 2020).

3.2 Empathy

The term empathy is used to explain a vast array of experiences. Emotion researchers normally define empathy as the capability to sense the emotions of other people, coupled with the ability to imagine what others might think or feel.

Contemporary researchers often distinguish between two types of empathy: "Affective empathy" refers to the sensations and feelings we get in response to the emotions of others; this can include mirroring what that person feels or simply feeling stressed when we detect the fear or anxiety of another. Cognitive empathy, sometimes called "perspective taking," means our ability to discover and understand the emotions of other people. Studies suggest a hard time empathizing with individuals with autism spectrum disorders.

Empathy has deep roots in our mind and bodies, and in the history of our evolution.

We have observed elementary forms of empathy in our primate relatives, in dogs, and even in rats. Empathy has been associated with two different brain pathways, and scientists have suggested that some elements of empathy can be traced to mirror cells in mind that fire when we view someone else undertake an action in much the same way they would fire if we perform that action ourselves.

Research has also revealed evidence of a genetic basis for empathy, though studies suggest that individuals can enhance (or restrict) their natural empathy.

Having empathy doesn't necessarily mean we are going to want to help someone in need, although it's often a vital first step towards compassionate action. Empathy is a building block of morality— for people to follow the Golden Rule, it helps if they are able to put themselves in the shoes of someone else. It is also a key ingredient in successful relationships because it helps us to understand other people's perspectives, needs, and intentions. Here are a few ways that research has shown the far-reaching importance of empathy.

Empathy is contagious

When group standards encourage empathy, people are more likely to be empathic — and more altruistic.

Empathy decreases prejudice and racism

in a study, white participants made to empathize with an African American man demonstrated less racial bias afterward from these early forms of empathy, research suggests that we can develop more complex forms that go a long way towards improving our relations and the world around us. Indeed, research suggests practicing awareness helps us take other people's perspectives while not feeling overwhelmed when we come across their negative emotions.

Get out of your own head:

Research shows that by actively imagining what another might experience, we can increase our own level of empathy.

Don't jump to conclusions about others:

We have less empathy when we believe that suffering people get what they deserve in some way.

Show empathic body language

Empathy is conveyed not only by what we say but also by our facial expressions, stance, tone of voice, and (or lack of) eye contact.

Meditate

Neuroscience research by Richard Davidson suggests that meditation— specifically loving-kindness meditation that focuses on concern for others— could increase the capacity for empathy among both short-term and long-term meditators (although particularly among long-term meditators).

Discover fantasy worlds: Keith Oatley and colleagues' research has found that people who read fiction are more attuned to the thoughts and actions of others.

Play games

Neuroscience research suggests our brains are making a "mental model" of the other person's thoughts and intentions when we compete against others.

Take baby lessons

The Roots of Empathy program by Mary Gordon is designed to boost empathy by bringing babies into classrooms, stimulating the basic instincts of children to resonate with the emotions of others.

Combating inequality Research has shown that achieving a higher socioeconomic status decreases empathy, perhaps because people with high SES have less need to connect, rely on, or cooperate with other people. As the difference between the haves and the have-nots widens, we also risk facing a gap in empathy. This does not mean that money is evil, but if you have a lot of it, you may need to be more willing to maintain your own empathy for others.

Pay attention to the faces

Pioneering research by Paul Ekman has found that by systematically studying facial expressions, we can improve our ability to identify the emotions of other people.

Believe empathy can be learned

People who think their level of empathy is evolving put more effort into being empathetic, listening to others, and helping even when it is difficult (What is Empathy?).

3.3 Motivation

People with high EI are prepared to defer immediate outcomes for long-term success. They are highly productive, love a challenge, and are effective at whatever they do.

Motivation is an in-house process. Either we define it as a drive or a necessity, motivation is a condition within us desiring a change, either in the self or the environment. Motivation pushes the person with the drive and direction needed to engage with the environment in an adaptive, open-ended, and problem-solving way when we tap into this well of energy (Reeve, 2018).

The essence of motivation is energized, and goal-directed behavior is persistent. When we're motivated, we take action and move.

Motivation is driven by fulfilling needs that are either necessary to sustain life or important to well-being and development. Food, water, and shelter physiological needs serve the organism to maintain life and also provide satisfaction.

Autonomy, mastery and belonging psychological needs direct our behavior in much the same way. Power, closure, meaning, and self-esteem as do the needs for achievement.

As with all the intrinsic activities we engage in, some of these needs will become motives.

In terms of extrinsic motivation, our environment and social context will play a significant role. We will also be motivated to experience specific emotions associated with certain end-state goals, values, and desires (Reeve, 2018).

Motivation is best explained when seeing what it feels like in everyday life. Here is an example of motivational reasons a person might have to engage in exercise. In psychology, the study of motivation is about providing the best possible answers to two major questions:

- What causes the particular behavior, and
- Why does behavior vary in intensity?

Motivational science is a science of behavior, which aims to construct hypotheses about what causes human motivation and how motivational mechanisms function.

When seen in the real world and evaluated by research, motivation is evident and measurable by behavior, commitment level, neural stimulation, and psychophysiology. Some will also include self-report in this list, but studies have shown that self-reporting sources of information have proved highly unreliable (Reeve, 2018). So how does motivation handle itself? With quality, intensity, and presence. Motivation is expressed through gestures and facial expressions, effort, immediacy (or like to be called short latency by psychologists).

It is possible to infer motivation from the levels of persistence and decision making in choosing one goal over another, which together make for a high probability of occurrence.

Motivation may also be inferred from the level of commitment.

Example, of a professional practitioner, will be actively and willingly contributing to the flow of interaction (agentic engagement), expressing interest and pleasure (emotional engagement), thinking intensely and paying attention (cognitive engagement) in a coaching scenario or motivational interview, and persisting in these efforts as if time and the outside world did not exist (behavioral engagement).

Motivation Model

In short, motives are internal experiences in the form of needs, cognition, and emotions, and they are the direct and proximal reasons of motivated action. Social and external events act as antecedents to motives that cause motivational states or trigger them. Our motives are expressed by behavior, commitment, psychophysiology, brain activation, and self-report.

Motivational psychologists study the motivation process and its components and attempt to find the answer to the questions about what causes motivation. It also shows why motivation research is so relevant to people's lives and how motivation leads positively to significant outcomes in life, such as success, efficiency, and well-being.

Motivation Process

Our motivation is often perceived as more immediate and powerful when it originates from internal motivations as categorized into needs, cognitions, and emotions

However, as we do not live in a vacuum, these inner interactions cannot take place without some degree of external influence, be it in the form of repercussions, rewards, or other types of pressure resulting from our environment's social context.

Our physiological and psychological needs are driving us, our cognitions are guiding us, and our activities are being driven by the emotions of land strength and energy.

When the combination of antecedent conditions and internal motives align, they create a ripe engagement environment that propels the behavior of the action.

In addition, when these behaviors produce more favorable motivational and emotional states, they reinforce actions by means of a positive feedback loop and increase the likelihood of repetition (Reeve, 2018).

Consider a motivational issue such as procrastination or avoidance.

Our needs, cognitions, emotions, surroundings, and relationships can play a crucial role in procrastination or avoidance.

All needs are born either from shortcomings or from the need for growth. Physiological requirements are an especially powerful factor in deciding behavior. For example, our bodies will signal our brain if our well-being is threatened, and this can lead to avoidance and procrastination if we suffer from hunger, thirst, or lack of sleep.

Psychological needs are also important drivers of motives, as they represent an inborn need to develop a sense of autonomy, competence, and connectedness. Such unconscious powers can be tough to overcome when we try to force ourselves to do something that meets those needs.

The conflict between the behavior chosen and the need to satisfy psychological needs, such as autonomy, can create dissonance, which can result in avoidance or procrastination. While the fulfillment of physiological desires is about maintaining health, it is about flourishing and developing as an individual to meet psychological needs

When in life, we are no longer able to change a particular situation, we are challenged to change ourselves.

There are also implicit needs that are acquired through socio-emotional development from our environment. They vary from individual to individual as our experiences vary, and implicit motives are acquired in contrast to inborn psychological needs. Implicit here means awkward. There is no conscious awareness of these needs, and they are trait-like and enduring. Implicit conditions inspire us to seek and fulfill specific social opportunities (Schultheiss & Brunstein, 2010).

An implicit motive is a psychological necessity resulting from situational indications that cause emotional reactions, which then predict, guide, and explain the behavior and lifestyle of people. They may be deduced from the characteristic thoughts, emotions, and behaviors of the person. What a person "needs" to experience a particular pattern of affect or emotion is an implicit motive.

For instance, if we have little or no need for accomplishment, we may experience negative effects such as shame, anxiety, and embarrassment while engaging in this challenging task and, as a result, avoid or delay. Implicit motives predict our behavior much more accurately than explicit motives, which are basically what we tell others about what motivates us.

Even our cognitions will influence our tendency to avoid or procrastinate. Cognitions are mental constructs such as goals, mentality, expectations, beliefs, and self-concept, to name a few who influence our motivation. For example, if we have conflicting goals, we may be more likely to avoid or procrastinate.

Emotions

Emotions, though closely linked to cognition and psychological needs, can be motivating or demotivating. They can signal that particular behavior is important.

We may feel joy or pride in achieving the goal by engaging in a particular behavior, or we may be afraid of failure and choose to avoid or shy away.

Our environment

Our environment can also be an ideal and supportive environment or an obstacle to staying motivated and achieving our goals. It can be full of distractions or conditions that enable sustained motivation.

Relationships

Finally, when it comes to change, our relationships can be supportive and empowering. This can be explained by a concept like a phenomenon in Michelangelo, where our relationships aid our potential. They can also be demotivating like in the phenomenon of Blueberry, where the relationship is the worst in us and can aid in procrastination and avoidance.

Motivation Cycle

Motivation is a dynamic process, and over time, our motives vary. Rising and falling as circumstances change, and motivations relate to the continuing cycle of behavior, as time passes. To complicate matters more, at any given point in time, we are motivated by a multitude of different motivations.

One motive, usually the most situationally appropriate one, will be strongest and dominate our attention while other motives will be relatively dormant and subordinate. While typically, the strongest motive will have the most considerable influence on our behavior as circumstances change, each subordinate motive can become dominant. The awareness of how motivation changes over time is especially important when it comes to setting goals.

When differentiating the motivational and performance-based advantages versus disadvantages for those who embrace a short-term goal, as eating less than 2000 calories today versus performers who embrace a long-term goal, such as losing 20 pounds this year, we need to consider the type of activity they engage in before making recommendations.

Short-term goals work better for uninteresting activities as they boost engagement by more frequently providing feedback on progress, further reinforcing efforts to persist (Reeve, 2018).

It is possible to improve motivation to perform routine or boring activities, however, by providing clarity of goals and choices on how to perform a task. Clarity and choice can feel a sense of superiority and control, and both can increase overall motivation in turn, as they meet basic psychological needs.

Long-term targets work better when it comes to fascinating projects, or as Mihaly Csikszentmihalyi (1990) calls them autotelic things, as they often have greater flexibility and more choice in how to execute these. Short term milestones for interesting activities can feel intrusive. Autotelic activities are engaging, and we are often intrinsically motivated to carry them out because they bring pleasure. But most importantly, in the absence of external rewards or incentives, we are motivated to pursue them. We need to keep in mind that motivation to act on the goals is often more when the goal is based in the coming future, while far-off goals do not build the tension of urgency that would motivate us to act immediately (Beata Souders, 2019)

3.4 Self-regulation

What Is Self-regulation?

Andrea Bell has a simple definition of self-regulation: it's "self-control" by self (2016).

As Bell also points out: "Whoever has good emotional self-regulation has the ability to keep its emotions in check. They can resist impulsive behaviors that could make their situation worse, and when they feel down, they can cheer themselves up. They have a flexible array of emotional and behavioral responses that are well suited to their environment's demands "(2016).

The goal of most therapy types is to improve the ability of an individual to self-regulate and to regain a feeling of control over one's behavior and life. When using the term "self-regulation," psychologists might refer to one of two things:

- Behavioral self-regulation or
- Emotional self-regulation.

We'll investigate the difference between the two below.

What is self-regulation with respect to behavior?

It is the ability to act in your best interests over the long term, in accordance with your deepest values" (Stosny, 2011). It's what lets us feel in one way but act in another.

If you've ever been afraid of getting up and going to work in the morning but convinced yourself to do so after remembering your goals (e.g., raising, promotion) or basic needs (e.g., food, shelter), you've shown effective self-regulation of behavior.

What Is Self-Regulation in Emotion?

On the other hand, emotional self-regulation involves controlling your emotions–or, at least, influencing them.

If you've ever spoken out of a bad mood or calmed down when you're angry, you've shown effective self-regulation of the emotions.

What is the theory of self-regulation?

The philosophy of self-regulation (SRT) clearly describes the mechanism and components involved in deciding what to think, feel, say, and do. It is particularly noteworthy when it comes to making a healthy choice when we have a strong wish to do the opposite, for example, not eating a whole pizza just because it tastes good.

There are four components involved, according to modern SRT expert Roy Baumeister (2007):

- Standards of desirable behavior,
- Motivation to meet standards,
- Monitoring conditions and thoughts that precede breaking standards, willpower allowing one's internal strength to control urges.

Those four components interact at any given moment to determine our self-regulatory activity. In words of SRT, our behavior is determined by the personal levels of good behavior, our motivation to meet those levels, the degree to which we are consciously aware of our circumstances and actions, and the extent to which we are willing to resist the temptations and choose the best course.

Self-regulation psychology

According to Albert Bandura, a self-efficacy expert, and leading SRT researcher, self-regulation is an ongoing process in which we:

- Monitor our behavior, the influences on our behavior, and the results of our behavior;
- Assess our behavior in relation to our own personal standards and broader, more contextual standards;
- Respond to our own behavior;

Bandura also states that self-efficacy plays a significant role and exerts its effect on our emotions, feelings, motives, and behavior.

A quick thought experiment can demonstrate the self-efficacy meaning: Imagine two people who are highly motivated to lose weight. They both monitor their dietary intake and exercise activities and have specific, measurable goals that they set for themselves.

One of them has a high degree of self-efficacy and assumes that he can lose weight if he puts effort into doing so. The other has low self-efficacy and feels he can't hold on to his prescribed weight loss plan.

Who do you think could better say no to desserts? Which one of them do you think will be more successful in getting up early every morning to exercise?

With reasonable certainty, we can say that the man with greater self-efficacy is likely to be more effective, even if both men begin with the exact same standards, motivation, monitoring, and willpower.

Another big name in SRT research, Barry Zimmerman, put forward his own self-regulated theory: self-regulated learning theory.

Self-regulated learning (SRL) refers to a student's process of taking responsibility for their own learning and applying themselves to academic success (Zimmerman, 2002).

This process takes place in three steps:

1. Planning: the student plans her/his task, sets goals, outlines strategies for tackling the task, and/or creates a schedule for the task;

2. Monitoring: at this stage, the student puts into action her plans and closely monitors her performance and experience with the methods she has chosen;

3. Reflecting: at last, after the task is complete and the results are in, the student's reaction to how she did that and why she did it the way she did.

By taking the initiative and regulating their own learning, students gain more deep insights into how they learn, what actions work best for them, and ultimately perform at a higher level. This improvement stems from the many learning opportunities during each phase:

1. During the planning phase, students have the opportunity to work on their self-assessment and learn how to choose the best strategies for success;

2. During the monitoring phase, students get the experience of implementing the strategies they have chosen and making real-time changes to their plans as necessary;

3. During the reflection phase, students synthesize everything they have learned and reflected on their experience, learning what is best for them, and what to change.

The Self-Regulatory System

To better understand SRT, it may be useful to consider the self-regulatory system. While the model is specific to health- and disease-related (rather than emotional) self-regulation, the complex processes at work during self-regulation of any kind remain a good representation.

Leventhal's Self-Regulatory System adapted from Hagger and Orbell (2003) describes how the system works: stimuli are introduced (i.e., something occurs that triggers a response, whether it's a thought, something said by another person, getting significant news, etc.); the individual makes sense of the stimuli, both cognitively (understanding) and emotionally (feeling);

Self-control and self-regulation

If you think that self-control and self-regulation have much in common, you're right. They are similar concepts, and some of the same processes they deal with. They are, however, two distinct structures.

As psychologist Stuart Shanker put it: Self-control is about inhibiting powerful impulses; self-regulation is about decreasing the frequency and intensity of extreme impulses by handling stress-load and recovery. Indeed, self-regulation is what makes self-control possible or, in many cases, unnecessary. "In this light, we can think of self-regulation as a process that is more automatic and subconscious (unless the individual determines to monitor or alter his or her self-regulation purposefully), while self-controlling is a set of purposeful decisions and behaviors.

Understanding the Depletion of Ego

An important concept of SRT is that of self-regulatory depletion, also called depletion of ego.

This is a state in which the willpower and control of an individual over self-regulation processes were used up, and the energy allocated for inhibiting impulses was expended. It often leads to poor decision-making and output (Baumeister, 2014).

When a person is confronted with many temptations (especially strong temptations), when it comes to controlling impulses, he or she must exert an equally powerful amount of energy. SRT argues that people have a limited will for this purpose, and once it's gone, two things happen:

1. Inhibitions and behavioral restraints are weaker, means that the person has less motivation and willingness to avoid temptations;

2. Temptations, needs, or urges are felt much more strongly when willpower is at a normal, undepleted level (Baumeister, 2014).

In SRT, that is a key idea. It describes why we struggle to avoid engaging in "bad conduct" when we are tempted by it for a long time. For example, it tells why many dieters can keep their strict diet all day, but when they are tempted by dessert, once they have dinner, they will give in.

It also describes why a married or otherwise committed person can reject an advance from someone who has not been their partner for days or weeks but who may eventually give in and have an affair.

Recent research in neuroscience supports this notion of self-regulatory depletion. A 2013 research by Wagner and colleagues used functional neuroimaging to demonstrate that individuals who had drained their self-regulatory capacity experienced reduced interaction between brain regions involved in self-control and rewards. In other words, despite prolonged self-regulatory behavior, their brains have been less helpful in helping them resist temptation.

Examples of self-regulatory behavior While self-regulatory depletion is a difficult hurdle, SRT does not imply that when your energy is depleted, it is impossible to remain in control of your urges and behaviors. It merely states that as your energy level drops, it becomes harder and harder.

There are, however, many examples of successful self-regulatory behavior, even when the individual is wary of consistent self-regulation.

Examples include

A cashier who will stay polite and calm when an angry customer berates him for the thing he has no control over;

A kid who refrains from throwing a tantrum when it is told that she cannot have the toy she eagerly wants;

A couple who are in an argument about something that is important for both of them to decide to take some time to cool off before continuing their discussion.

As you can see, self-regulation encompasses a wide range of behaviors from minute-to-minute choices to larger, more meaningful decisions that can have a significant impact on whether we are meeting our objectives.

Why self-regulation is vital for the well-being

Let's take a closer view at how self-regulation helps us improve and maintain a healthy sense of well-being.

Overall, tons of evidence suggests that those who successfully display self-regulation enjoy greater well-being in their everyday behavior. Researchers Skowron, Holmes, and Sabatelli (2003) found a positive link between greater self-regulation and health for both men and women.

For youth research, the results are similar. A 2016 study showed that teenagers who regularly engage in self-regulatory actions report greater well-being than their peers, including increased life satisfaction, perceived social support, and optimism (i.e., good feelings) impact

besides, those who suppressed their feelings rather than tackling them head-on experienced lower well-being, including greater loneliness, more negative effects (i.e., bad feelings), and worse overall psychological health (Verzeletti, Zammuner, Galli, Agnoli, & Duregger, 2016).

Emotional Intelligence and Well-being

To become more specific, one of the ways in which self-regulation contributes to well-being is through emotional intelligence.

Self-regulation, or the extent of a person's ability to influence or control his or her emotions and impulses, is an important piece of emotional intelligence, and it is easy to see why: Can you imagine someone with a high level of self-awareness, motivation and social skills but limited control on his or her impulse is driven by uninhibited emotion.

Because of the important role of self-regulation in emotional intelligence, there is something off about that picture. Yet emotional intelligence, as researchers Di Fabio yet Kenny have found, is closely linked to well-being (2016).

The better we understand and address our emotions and other people's emotions, the better we make sense of our environments, adapt to them, and pursue our objectives (Ackerman, 2019).

3.5 Social skills

People with strong social competencies are usually team players. Besides focusing on their own success, they help others evolve and shine. They can manage disputes, they are excellent networkers, and they master relationship building and maintaining.

Chapter 4: Improving your emotional intelligence

Emotional intelligence drives your workplace and personal performance, but it starts with you. From your trust, empathy, and motivation to your social competencies and self-control, knowing and controlling your own emotions will improve progress in all areas of your life.

Whatever professional field you're in, whether you're running a two or twenty or even just yourself, it's a great starting point to realize how effective you're in controlling your own emotional energy. Emotional intelligence, absent from the curriculum, is not something that we are taught or evaluated on, so where did it originate, do you have it, and is it really so important?

Luckily, it's something you can learn, and we've assembled a detailed list of tips to help you discover your own level of emotional intelligence and develop valuable emotional intelligence skills that can be incorporated into daily life.

4.1 Ways to improve emotional intelligence

1) Observe how you feel

Often we lead a busy, hectic lifestyle, and it's too easy for us to lose touch with our emotions. Attempt to reconnect, during the day, to set a timer for different points. Taking a few deep breaths when the timer goes off and remember how you feel emotionally. Pay attention to where that emotion shows up in your body as a physical sensation, and how it feels. The more you practice, the more of a second nature it becomes.

#2) Be careful how you behave

While practicing your emotional awareness, take the time to notice your behavior as well.

Observe how you behave when you feel those feelings, and how this affects your daily life. Managing our emotions gets easier when we become more aware of how we respond to them.

#3) Question your own views

In this hyper-related world, it's easy to fall into a' bubble of opinion.' This is a state of existence where people with similar viewpoints are constantly reinforcing your own opinions. Take your time to read the other side of the story and challenge your views (even if you still feel they're right). This will help you to understand others and to be more responsive to new ideas.

#4) Take responsibility for your feelings

Your emotions and behaviors come from you, they don't come from anyone else, and once you begin to take responsibility for your feelings and behaviors, they will have a positive impact on all areas of your life.

#5) Take time to celebrate the good moments

One key part of emotional intelligence celebrates and reflects on the good moments in life. People with positive emotions are generally more resilient and are more likely to have fulfilling relationships, which will help them move past adversity.

#6) don't ignore the negative

Reflecting on negative sentiments is as important as reflecting on the positive. Knowing why you feel negative is crucial to becoming a fully-rounded person who will be more able to deal with negative issues in your life in the future.

7) Don't forget to breathe

Life throws different situations our way, with most of us regularly experiencing some sort of stress.

Do not forget to breathe to control the emotions when that happens and to prevent outbursts. Call a time out and go wash your face with cold water, go outside and get some fresh air or make a drink–anything that keeps you calm and gives you a chance to hold on to what's going on and how you should react.

#8) Lifetime cycle

Consider and note that emotional intelligence is something you build and needs continuous improvement; it's very much a lifelong practice.

#9) Learn to look at yourself objectively

Understanding yourself fully is daunting, and it's almost impossible to look at yourself objectively, so feedback from those who know you is essential. Tell them where the strengths and weaknesses lie, write down, and compare what they suggest. Watch out for any trends and remember not to disagree with them–that doesn't mean that they're right–they're just trying to help you gauge your experience from another's viewpoint.

#10) keep a journal

A great way to get an accurate gage of yourself is by keeping a diary. Start by writing what happened to you every day, how you feel, and how you treated it. Documenting such details will make you more aware of what you are doing and highlight where problems might come from. Check your feedback regularly, and take note of any patterns.

#11) Understand what motivates you

When you start a project, everybody has a central motivation. The challenge, as adversity arises, is to keep this driving force in mind.

All too often, people are starting a project but failing to complete it because they are losing their drive.

Take time to understand and use what motivates you to push you across the finish line.

#12) Take it easy

Sometimes there are emotional explosions because we don't take the time to slow down and evaluate how we feel. Give yourself a break, and meditate, do yoga or read–wonders work a little escapism. And then try to pause before you react, the next time you have an emotional reaction to something.

#13) Recognize your emotional triggers.

Individuals who are conscious of themselves can recognize their emotions as they occur. Being flexible with your emotions and tailoring them to your situation is important. Don't deny the stage time of your emotions, but also don't be rigid with them, take the time to process your feelings before communicating them.

#14) Predict how you feel

Think of a situation you're going into and predict how you're going to feel. Practice naming sentiments and accepting them- naming the feeling puts you in control. Try choosing a suitable response to the feeling rather than just reacting to it.

#15) Trust your intuition

If you're still unsure of the path to follow, trust your intuition. After all, your subconscious has learned which path to take throughout your whole life

#16) come out of it

One good way to keep your emotions in check is to change your sensory input–as the old saying goes, motion dictates emotion. So jolt your body out of routine by attending an exercise class or attempting to channel a busy mind with a game like a puzzle or a book-anything to break your existing routine.

#17) Keep a schedule (and stick to it!)

Making sure you're creating a schedule and sticking to it is extremely important if you want to complete tasks well.

Paul Minors of Productivities writes "When you schedule appointments in your calendar, you say to yourself: 'I'm going to do A, B and C by X date and it's going to take Y hours.' Once you make that promise, it's getting harder to procrastinate.'

#18) Eat well

This seems an easy one, but watching what you eat and drink can have a big impact on your emotional state, so try your best.

#19) Don't get your emotional energy mad

Put your energy into productive things. It's good to keep overwhelming emotions inside, particularly when letting them out isn't an appropriate time. But instead of venting it on something futile when you do, turn it into motivation instead. Don't get mad; make things better.

#20) Be interested

A major factor in managing yourself and your emotions, whether business or personal, is constantly taken out time to be interested in the subject matter.

#21) don't expect from others to trust you if you don't trust people

It can be difficult to establish trust with a person, and once it's lost, it can be very difficult to regain. Try to be aware that people are just human and that they will make mistakes. You invite people to offer their trust in return by offering your trust.

#22) Personal goals

Personal goals can provide long-term guidance and encouragement in the short term. So hold a pen and paper and think about where you want to be, and set yourself some goals. Based on your strengths, and make them relevant to you, make them fun and realistic. in the end, That task alone is enough to get you motivated instantly!

#23) Be realistic

When setting a new goal, be sure to set realistic and clear goals for yourself to achieve that goal and understand that change is an inevitable part of life. Achievement boosts Confidence, and so does the ability to achieve more; see how it works, as self-confidence rises?

#24) Positive thinking

It's significant to maintain a positive and optimistic attitude to keep motivated. Consider challenges and losses as learning opportunities rather than failures, and try to avoid negative people and choose to surround yourself with optimistic, well-motivated people–they will have a great impact on you.

#25) Lifelong learning

Both knowledge and information are vital to feeding your mind and keeping you informed and motivated. And with knowledge so easily accessible, at the click of a button, you have the ability to fuel your beliefs and passions!

#26) Be prepared to come out of your comfort zone

The greatest obstacle to achieving your full potential is not to challenge yourself so often enough. If you're ready to come out of your comfort zone, great things can happen to you, so do as often as you can.

#27) Ask for Help

Don't be afraid when you need to ask for help and vice versa. If others need assistance, don't hold back in offering them help. Watching others excel will only help motivate yourself.

#28) Stand and stretch

Take a stand and stretch as far as you can for 10 seconds for an instant short-term boost to your motivation. Once you return to your office, you're going to be in the right frame of mind and ready to work.

#29) Listen before you can empathize with someone

You need to first understand what they're thinking, which means listening is at the very epicenter of empathy. This means encouraging them to speak without interference, preconceptions, cynicism, and pause your own issues so you can absorb their condition and understand how they feel before you respond.

#30) Try to be approachable

Whether you're the team leader or working with others on a project, try to stay accessible and accessible.

#31) Perspective

We're all familiar with the phrase "position yourself in your shoes," and that's exactly what it means. The simplest way to gain a little perspective when a question or situation arises next time is to exchange places with that person and think about what's going on from his or her point of view. There is sometimes no right or wrong, but at least you will understand enough to come to a solution or offer some useful advice.

4.2 Signs of High Emotional Intelligence

1. You think in terms of feelings.

Emotional intelligence begins with what you and others call self-and social awareness, the ability to recognize emotions (and their impact).

That consciousness starts with reflection. You ask questions such as: What are my emotional powers? What are my failings?

How does my current mood affect the way I think and make decisions?

What's going on beneath the surface, influencing what others are saying or doing?

Asking such questions yields valuable insights that can be used to your advantage.

2. You take a break.

The pause is as simple as having to stop for a moment and think before you speak or act. (Easy in theory, difficult in practice.) That can help save you from embarrassing moments or committing too fast.

To put it another way, pausing helps you avoid making a permanent decision based on a temporary emotion.

3. You strive to get your thoughts under control.

You have little control over the emotion that you feel in a given moment. But you can have control of your reaction to those emotions— with your thoughts focused. (As it has been said: You cannot prevent a bird from landing on your head, but you can prevent it from making a nest.) By trying to control your thoughts, you oppose becoming a slave of your emotions, allowing yourself to live in a way that is in line with your objectives and values.

4. You take advantage of the criticism.

No-one is enjoying negative feedback. But you know critique is an opportunity to learn, even if it is not delivered in the best possible way. And even if it's unfounded, it gives you a glimpse of how others think.

You keep your emotions in check when you receive negative feedback, and ask yourself: How can this make me better?

5. They exhibit authenticity.

Authenticity does not mean sharing every little thing about yourself, all the time, to everyone. It means saying what you mean, what you think, what you say, and above all, sticking to your values and principles.

You know not everyone will appreciate the sharing of your feelings and thoughts. But whoever matters will.

6. They show empathy.

The ability to display empathy that includes understanding the thoughts and feelings of others helps you to connect with others. You are working hard to see things through their eyes, instead of judging or labeling others.

Empathy does not necessarily mean consenting to the point of view of another person. Rather, it's about trying to understand— which allows you to build relationships deeper and more connected.

7. They love others.

All human beings yearn for recognition and appreciation. If you commend others, you will satisfy that craving and build Confidence in the process.

All of this starts when you focus on the good in others. Then you inspire them to be the best version of themselves by sharing specifically what you appreciate.

8. They provide useful feedback.

Negative feedback has huge potential to hurt other people's feelings. You reframe criticism as constructive feedback to realize this, so the recipient sees it as helpful rather than harmful.

9. They apologize when they are wrong

It takes guts and strength to be able to say you are sorry. But doing so shows humility, a quality that naturally will draw others to you.

Emotional intelligence helps you realize that excuse does not always mean that you are wrong. It does mean your relationship is valued more than your ego.

10. They forgive and forgot.

Leaving a knife inside a wound is like hanging on to resentment. While the offending party is moving on with their lives, you never give yourself an opportunity to heal.

By forgiving and forgetting, you prevent others from holding their emotions hostage — allowing them to move forward.

11. They stick to your obligations.

It is common for people nowadays to break a deal or commitment when they feel like it. Of course, bailing with a friend on a Netflix evening will cause less harm than breaking your child's promise or missing a major business deadline.

But you develop a strong reputation for reliability and trustworthiness when you make a habit of keeping your word — in big and small things-.

12. Help others.

One of the greatest ways of having a positive impact on others ' emotions is to help them.

Most people don't really care about where you graduated from, or even what you've achieved before. But what about the hours you are willing to take for listening or helping out of your schedule? Your readiness to get down and work alongside them in the trenches?

Such actions build Confidence and inspire others to follow your lead when it counts.

13. They guard themselves against emotional sabotage.

You know that emotional intelligence also has a dark side — such as when people try to manipulate the feelings of others in order to promote a personal agenda or for some other selfish cause (Bariso, 2018).

4.3 How to Give Negative Feedback That Is Emotionally Smart

It's time to throw the sandwich away. Here's how to count up your feedback.

Over the years, managers and leaders have been trained using the sandwich method to give feedback. You start by sharing something positive, followed by (hopefully) constructive criticism, and end on a positive note once again.

Something like that often goes like this:

John: something I wanted to talk to you about, Jenny. You've done some really positive things lately, first of all.

Jenny: (Thinking — OK; now what did I do? Brace yourself)

John: [a relatively positive thing], but I wanted to mention something else as well.

Jenny: here it starts

John: [Criticism, preceded by an uncomfortable pause.] But you're doing a good job overall, too. Thank you!

Jenny: Okay. You will welcome (Jerk.)

Where did all of this go wrong?

The Issue

If you've ever been on this rotten sandwich's receiving end, then you know it's not very effective. So why do so many people feel tempted to use it?

Many managers give negative feedback and are uncomfortable. If they keep things (mostly) positive, they feel the process becomes easier to bear, and the person who receives the negative feedback won't hate them.

But the person getting this type of feedback usually tunes in at the beginning, and the end anything good said. Why? For what? It is just flapping. They know the deal: they did something wrong, and that's all they care about this conversation (and they'll remember from it). The positive feedback is gasping.

But it is also people who need positive feedback. A sense of appreciation is a powerful motivator. A culture that supports truthful and specific praise is doing employee engagement wonders. (More on that here.) So how are you doing the right thing?

The solution to this is.

The key to effective, emotionally smart feedback is the separate delivery of positive and negative messages.

How are you?

1. Give the right time to praise and criticize.

Any feedback— positive or negative— is best shared as soon as possible, according to research cited in the Harvard Business Review.

This makes sense; you don't wait for wrong behavior to be corrected; if you do, you risk minimizing the effect of what happened or forgetting to say something completely.

But you need to look at praise the same way: tell the person as soon as possible if you see something you like. If you cannot do it right away, make a note, or set a reminder to make sure that you don't forget.

There should be a balance in the feedback. Look to praise positive actions and behaviors. On the same note, quickly share constructive criticism after you have noticed something negative. You can be absolutely direct, no sandwich feedback. At other, more appropriate times, you have given positive reinforcement, so they will know you are simply looking for their best interests.

2. Be specific and be honest.

Do not just say "Good job" when you praise someone; tell them what they are doing right, and why you appreciate it. If you are struggling to find a point to commend, think about ways in which the person has been faithful to the company, or has been persistent with him or herself. It is your job to see the good points of the employees, as well as their potential. There is something that everyone deserves to be praised for.

Do the same as wrong. Don't just tell people what they did wrong, but how they can improve. Give them the chance to answer when sharing your concerns. Be open to the possibility that you missed something, or even contribute to a damaging situation in some way.

Build a culture where other people feel comfortable to give you negative feedback when needed.

How to Start

How do you start the conversation if you're not sandwiching the negative between the positive ones?

Take one example. Though well prepared, there were some major flaws in Jenny's presentation. You might start by doing the following when you meet her: "Jenny, I wanted to talk to you about your presentation. How did you feel about it? Did you find anything particularly challenging?" By listening carefully to Jenny's answer, you can tailor your feedback to her specific needs. Then you might ask something like, "Would you be willing to hear some constructive criticism?" After tactfully sharing your comments and suggestions, you conclude by thanking Jenny for taking the time to meet you and for being ready to listen. You also show that you hope it proves helpful.

The foregoing is not a specific formula, just an example of how you could do it.

Authenticity is important, so you should make it your own. Hopefully, it's a starting point.

If you can master these techniques, you will use emotional intelligence to guide and mentor your subordinates. In the end, they'll appreciate you making them better.

Chapter 5: Raising kids with High EQ

Self-awareness, emotional attunement to others, and knowing one's own emotional state, are several attributes that belong to a high-QE individual. A child who is self-conscious, has insight and is considerate about the feelings of others is often a child who is emotionally intelligent and on the way to having a high EQ.

Such general capacities such as gratitude, thoughtfulness, empathy, and kindness give rise to a multitude of positive emotional qualities. A child who is in contact with his or her emotions may be a child who can identify a state of feeling, rather than acting it out inappropriately.

It's natural for a child to have an occasional meltdown, a lapse in appreciation, or self-absorbed moment, but most children with a healthy emotional constitution regularly exhibit conscientious abilities in the context of a close relationship.

"Thank you," "I'm sorry," "I made an error," or "Are you all right? "A child who rarely says these without a prompt may lack the greater emotional skills that enable a person to attain emotional intelligence eventually.

Too often, a parent makes a child for showing appreciation, responsibility, or empathy. "They're just a kid." This could be an extreme error. Character is early established, and the correlation between a secure attachment to a caregiver and emotional intelligence is evidence that a child can exhibit these qualities at a young age. These characteristics, when fostered, can result in a child having healthy emotional regulation, emotional intelligence, and, ultimately, a high EQ.

A secure attachment is formed when an infant\toddler experiences an emotionally tuned caregiver, who responds to him or her empathetically.

Moreover, a parent who is capable of admitting fault within the parent-child dyad context actually allows a child to experience self-awareness and accountability within the attachment relationship. "I am sorry that I have lost my patience. I definitely frightened you. I like it. "These are examples of a parent in a relationship with a child taking ownership of his or her errors.

When a caregiver displays self-awareness, accountability, and understanding in the relationship between parent and child, the child has a chance to experience and internalize these emotionally intelligent qualities. Conversely, a parent who thinks he or she is never wrong may unintentionally discourage a child from incorporating valuable emotionally intelligent skills when he or she makes a mistake and is unaware of a child's feelings. In fact, a parent who shames a child for having a feeling that varies from how the parent feels can also be an obstacle to emotional growth for the child.

Though the child's empathy experience is what enables him or her to naturally embody the ability, the difference between an empathic parent and a parent that enables is critical. If a parent is too compassionate and is sorry for a child (sympathy), the parent may be compelled to break the rules, lower or give up standards. Unfortunately, this teaches a child to play the victim, to deflect and blame for the project, and to manipulate to get what it wants. The trick is empathizing, not sympathizing, and keeping expectations. Examples are: "You're mad. I can see, but you can't have your backpack thrown. Please go and pick it up." "You are unable to do it. I get it, but, honey, don't quit. Hold on, trying." "You're worried. I understand it is difficult. But you could do it. "It's hurtful to see someone do something you want to do, but they can't. I do. I get it. But your friend can't take it out. Excuse me, please.

5.1 How to increase Emotional Intelligence in kids

So, you want to raise an emotionally smart child, and you wonder where to start? Start with those five steps.

1. Recognize the viewpoint and empathize with your kids.

Even if you can't "do anything" about the upsets of your child, sympathize with that. Just being heard helps people relinquish disturbing feelings. If the upset of your child seems out of proportion with the situation, remember that all of us store up emotions and then let us experience them once we find a safe haven. We are then free to move on.

Empathizing doesn't mean you're in agreement, just that you to see it from his side. He may have to do what you're saying, but he has the right to his own view. We know how good it feels to have our position acknowledged; when we don't get our way, it just makes it easier.

"It's difficult for you to quit playing and come for dinner, but now is the time." "You hoped you could have me all to yourself, right? "You're so disappointed that it's raining." "I know you want to stay up later, like the big kids." "Your tower fell mad! "Why this promotes emotional intelligence: feeling understood activates calming biochemical; the neural pathway you activate if you feel soothed is what you use to soothe yourself as you grow older.

By experiencing it from others, children develop Empathy.

You help your child reflect on his or her experience, and what triggers his or her feelings. For the little ones, just knowing that their feeling has a name is an early tool in learning how to manage the emotions that flood them.

2. Allow them to express themselves

One cannot distinguish between their emotions and their "self." Accept the emotions of your child rather than deny or minimize them, which gives children the message that certain feelings are shameful or unacceptable.

Rejecting her fear or anger will not stop her from having those sentiments, but it may well force her to repress. Unfortunately, repressed feelings don't fade away, as freely expressed feelings do. They are trapped, and they seek a way out. Because they're not under conscious control, when a child socks her sister, has nightmares or develops a nervous tic, they pop out unmodulated.

Instead, teach that the full range of emotions is understandable and part of being human, even though certain actions need to be limited.

"You are so furious that your brother broke your toy! I understand, AND it's never all right to hit, even if you're very mad. Tell your brother how you feel, in words.

"You look worried about today's field trip. On-field trips, I used to get nervous, too, in kindergarten. Want to tell me this?" You're so frustrated! Does nothing seem to go right for you this morning I wonder if you just need to cry? Sometimes everyone needs to cry. Come hug Daddy, and you can cry as much as you want your acceptance helps your child accept her feelings, which is what allows us to solve our feelings and move on, so she's better able to get on with them.

Your acceptance teaches your child that there is no danger to her emotional life, that she is not shameful, and that she is universal and manageable. She finds out she isn't alone. She knows that even the less pleasant parts of herself are acceptable, meaning she's completely ok, just the way she is.

3. Listen to your kids.

Remember that rage doesn't start dissipating until it feels heard. Whether your child is five months or sixteen months old, she needs you to listen to the feelings that she expresses. She will let them go, and get on with her life once she feels and expresses them. You'll be surprised at how cooperative and affectionate she'll be once she's given the opportunity to show you how she feels. But she needs to know that you are fully present and listening to feel safe to let those feelings go up and out. Ensured its safe, kids have an incredible ability to let their feelings wash over and out, leaving them relaxed and cooperative. Do you have a job? Breathe through it, stay present, and oppose the urge to let go of those troubled feelings. Your child knows instinctively how to cure herself.

"Right now, you sound so unhappy. Sometimes, everybody gets upset I'm here, right now. Tell me about it." "You're so sad and mad. You just want to scream and cry and shout. Often, everyone feels that way. I'm listening right here and seeing all those great feelings. You can show me just how insane and sad you are.

"You're so mad you're screaming at me to leave. I am going to move back a little bit. But those feelings hurt and scare you, and with these disturbing feelings, I'm not going to leave you alone. I am here now, and you are free. You can be as mad as you want to, and I'm right here to hug you when you're ready. "Why this promotes emotional intelligence: The essence of healthy human emotions is to flow through us, overwhelm us, and then pass away. Instead of finding healthy expression, emotions get stuck inside us when we repress them. But children are terrified that they are overwhelmed by their strong emotions, so they try to fend them off unless they feel safe enough to face them. Since feelings are contained in the body, tantrums are a way of helping young children wind up in nature.

In making our children feel secure enough to feel and express their emotions, we are not only restoring their psyches and bodies; we are encouraging them to trust their own emotional cycle so that they can manage their feelings as they grow older, without tantrums or suppression.

4. Teach them problem-solving

Emotions are messages, not wallowing mud. Teach your kid to breathe through them, feel and tolerate them without having to act on them, and, if necessary, when they are not in the grip of strong emotion, to solve problems and act.

Most of the time, once children (and adults) feel that their emotions are understood and accepted, they lose their charge and start dissipating. That leaves an opening to solve problems. Children can do this themselves, at times. They need your help sometimes to brainstorm. But oppose the urge to rush in and handle the situation for them unless they ask you to; this gives him the message you don't trust his ability to handle it himself.

"You are so disappointed that, because she is sick, Molly can't come over. You were really eager to play with her. Perhaps we can brainstorm ideas of something else when you're ready to do that sounds like fun." "You're pretty irritated with Sam not giving you a turn. Sometimes you feel like you no longer want to play with him. But you really enjoy playing with him too. What could you say, Sam, I wonder, so he could know how you feel? "Why this encourages emotional intelligence: children must express their feelings, but they must also know how to shift gears in order to find constructive solutions to problems. On our part, that takes practice and modeling.

Research shows that empathizing with our children is simply not enough to teach them how to manage their feelings, as they still feel at the mercy of their emotions.

Teaching kids to honor their emotions as signals about things they need to handle in their lives in a different way empowers children.

All kids need coaching to learn how to express their needs without attacking someone else.

5. Play it out

Realize that your child has some big feelings when you notice a negative pattern developing, she doesn't know how to handle it, and step in with the best medicine: play. For example, your four-year-old might always want Mommy, for example. Help him work through his feelings like how much he prefers Mom by playing a game where poor bumbling Dad "tries" unsuccessfully to keep him away from her rather than taking it personally. Dad gets between his mother and son, and roars, "I'm not going to let you get to Mom Hey, and you just ran around me! You have just pushed me over! You're too forceful! But you are not going to get past me this time! "Your four-year-old giggles and boasts and gets a chance to prove that he can EVER have his mother. He will also unload all those pent-up worries that make him ask her.

Why this promotes emotional intelligence: On a daily basis, all children experience big feelings. They often feel powerless, angry, sad, scared, or jealous, and pushed about. Those feelings are being processed with play by emotionally healthy children, which is how little ones of all species learn. Helping your child "play" out his big internal conflicts lets him solve them so that he can move on to the next developmental challenge that is appropriate for his age.

Your child cannot put his deeper emotional conflicts into words; even for most adults, that is tough. But he can symbolically play them out and resolve them without even talking about them.

Laughter releases both stress hormones and tears — and is a lot more fun.

5.2 Emotional Intelligence Teaching when Emotions Run High

The most well-intentioned parent can be triggered when storm clouds brew, and escalate the upset rather than calm it down. But when your child wrests with human emotions that are more "difficult," he needs your help to learn how to fix them. This is the most crucial time to teach emotional intelligence— meaning to help your child develop the ability to soothe himself, regulate his feelings, and get along with others. Here are ways to help your child build a smarter brain each day.

1. Respond to the needs and feelings behind the conduct of problems.

Kids want to have warm, happy interactions with their parents. They want people to be "good." Misbehavior originates from overwhelming feelings or unfulfilled needs. If you do not address the emotions and needs, they will just burst out later, causing another behavior that is problematic. Examples of listening to needs: Connection: "It's hard to let go of myself this morning. Starting school was fun, but you're losing time with Mommy. I'm going to be right here to pick you up after school, and we're going to snuggle and play together and have some special time, okay?" Good sense of power/agency: "It looks like you want to do this yourself! I'm right here if you need support." But when you help them settle in on their inner experience and give them language to express their desires, they get better at understanding themselves and learning how to speak for themselves in a suitable way.

2. Accept all feelings, even though you restrict your behavior.

Of course, you have to limit the actions of your child. He can't run down the street, throw his dinner on the floor, hit his sister, or play all night on the computer. Set a limit in every situation where the conduct of your child is obviously unacceptable. (If it's not "clear" whether the behavior is acceptable to you, just ask yourself if you're okay to be flexible and make sure you're not pushing yourself past your own level of comfort.) But even while you're limiting behavior, your child is allowed to have and express all her emotions, including feelings of disappointment or anger, in response to your limitations. Kids need to "show" us how they feel and have us "hear" them, and meltdowns are the release valve of nature for the emotions of kids. Besides banishing your child to her room for control (which gives her the message that she's all alone with those big, frightening feelings), hold her or stay close and connected to your soothing voice: "You seem so sad right now. I'm right here; you're safe." Once the storm has passed, your child will be willing to cooperate and affectionate, and feel so much more connected to you. During a meltdown, disregard any anger or rudeness; your child is showing you the depth of her upset. The time to teach is after the hurricane, not during. And you will find that, once you help your child with her feelings, not much teaching is really necessary. That's because she knows the expected behavior already; she simply couldn't control those big emotions. The first phase in her mastering the ability is your calming support.

Why this encourages emotional intelligence: It starts dissipating when we let ourselves feel an emotion. But when we try to push the feelings out of our consciousness, it isn't going away. We are actually losing the ability to manage that. So the first step in learning how to regulate emotions is to enable them to become conscious of them.

When we tell children that all feelings are all right, they are friendly with their emotions rather than stuffing them up. That would allow them to start self-regulating.

When children are capable of managing their feelings, they may regulate their behavior.

3. Regulate your own feelings.

Children will not always do what you say but will always do what you do, eventually. Children learn from us about emotional regulation. This tells our child when we stay calm that there is no emergency, even if she feels like there is at the moment.

Of course, when you are running on empty, you cannot remain calm. That's why one of our most important parenting responsibilities is to maintain our own sense of wellbeing.

Most of us keep this relatively well together until our child gets upset. Remember, you don't have to "fix" the frustration of your child or suppress the feelings of your child. On the contrary, just accept what they feel and keep your own balance.

The other time many parents get upset as their kids get upset and start disciplining their child. But staying calm, and seeing the perspective of your child as you set limits, is especially important. There is no reason whatsoever for blame or punishment, which will shame children and make them more misbehave. Look for firm boundaries, set with empathy: "I'm sorry, Luis, I know it's hard to quit. It's sleeping time now, and you can play tomorrow. Now it's time to say goodbye, Game. Okay, I'm turning it off. I see that makes you sad. You want you to be able to play all night, every night, don't you? Come, let's be sure we have enough time for a tale.

When we set limits with a sense of the perspective of the child, the child is less likely to resist the limits. Once children give up what they want to meet our boundaries, they're creating the self-regulating neural pathways.

4. Remember that anger, like fear, hurt, or sadness, is always a defense against deeper emotions.

He isn't rude when your child is expressing anger. He's defending himself against feeling hurt or fear at those more vulnerable emotions. Recognize the anger of your child, but then go beneath it to empathize with the deeper emotions that spur the anger. Feeling those deeper emotions will melt the wrath of your kid.

What does "Hate" mean? Don't be sad. Your kid just throws at you the nuclear option to show you how upset he is. Hate is by no means a feeling, but a "position," or a stance that we assume to protect ourselves. Empathize as if your child is simply expressing his or her anger. Do you mean that you hate this new baby? I'm listening. You get really mad at her sometimes just for being here. And for spending time with the baby, I see how mad you are at me too. When it was just us, you liked it better. You feel so sad now that things are different and I'm so busy with the boy. Come hug me, and I will hold you up, and you'll be able to tell me your feelings of sadness and madness. I'm going to kiss your nose and toes when you're ready, and we can play baby games, just you and me, just like we did when you were a kid. As many parents had frightening encounters with anger as young children, we're still scared of the anger of our children.

5. Have expectations that cannot be fulfilled

It's almost dinner time, but you cannot wait. Let's make a snack that makes your body feel better. "Why this promotes emotional intelligence: we all have expectations that cannot be fulfilled.

Having a variety of ways to manage such desires, as well as other needs and emotions, is an important tool to cope with the emotional intelligence toolkit of any kid.

6. Do not take it personally and resist the urge to intensify or react

"It's about your child: their tangled feelings, their difficulty in self-control, their immature ability to understand and express their emotions. You never understand!" try to listen that as information about her— she feels like she has never understood it at this moment— rather than about you. Remember, it is hard to be a child. He still doesn't have the inner strength to control her emotions— but you are, right?

Why this enhances emotional intelligence: Our job as adults is always to calm, rather than escalate, the emotional storm, how else will our child learn to do so on their own?

You're showing when you're emotionally generous to your kid that she's not flawless, but you love her anyway— even when she's at her worst. That is the unconditional love every child needs to thrive.

Crazy? Sure, because most of us find that controlling our own feelings is difficult so that we can accept the unruly emotions of our children.

5.3 Importance of Teaching EI in Schools

Improving mental health, social skills, learning outcomes, and have an enduring impact on children that can last a long time.

Children focus on enhancing their school intelligence through math, science, reading, and writing activities and lessons, but are your children also learning to become smarter emotionally at school?

Emotional Intelligence Quotient (EQ) is the capacity to recognize, direct, and express emotions in a positive way. It is a powerful technique that can help kids understand themselves better, overcome challenges, and build strong relationships throughout their lives with others. People with high EQ tend to tolerate and manage difficult feelings such as sadness, anger, and fear. Fortunately, EQ is an easily learnable skill.

In the last 15 to 20 years, EQ programs have become more common in schools. These programs, known as social and emotional learning (SEL), help children focus on thinking, behavioral, and regulatory skills, which they need to communicate effectively with others. According to a new study at the University of Illinois and Loyola University, SEL youth programs not only quickly improve mental health, social skills, learning outcomes, and prosocial behaviors (such as kindness, sharing, and empathy) but also have an ongoing benefit for the children that can last many years to come.

In reality, according to the report, students who participated in SEL programs graduated from college at a rate of 11 percent higher and from secondary school at a rate six percent higher. In comparison, substance use and behavioral problems for participants in the SEL system were six percent lower, crime rates 19 percent lower, and mental health condition diagnoses 14.5 percent less.

The study analyzed that from 82 different SEL programs involving 97,406 kindergarten students through high school in the USA, Europe, and the UK. The researchers assessed the impacts at least six months after completion of the programs. Researchers found that social-emotional learning had positive effects in the classroom, but was also correlated with positive outcomes over the longer term. Those advantages were identical regardless of the race, socioeconomic background, or position of the school students.

Social-emotional learning programs are so critical since they offer the skills to help students succeed later in life. They teach kids how to recognize and understand their emotions, feel empathy, make decisions, build relationships, and maintain them. Previous studies have shown that integrating these programs into the classroom enhances learning outcomes and decreases student anxiety and behavioral problems. Study researchers believe that teaching social-emotional learning in schools is an effective way to give kids the experiences and strategies they need to be successful in life. It may even end up encouraging better outcomes for public health. The researchers suggest that such skills should be developed over time and incorporated easily into the curriculum of regular schools. How important it is in schools for social-emotional learning to take place because this approach will affect all kinds of children, including poor ones. Most children spend more than 900 hours each year at school, so what they learn with their peers in school can often have a bigger effect than what their families tell them, particularly as they get older in middle and high school.

Some of the SEL services that are most popular include Mind up and Roots of Empathy. They focus on developing the following key competencies: self-consciousness, self-management, social awareness, relationship skills, and responsible decision-making.

5.3 How Teachers can help in Improving Emotional Intelligence in Kids

Many educators incorporate social and emotional learning (SEL) programs into the curriculum. These programs are effective not only in improving the emotional intelligence of students but also in preventing bullying and increasing academic success.

Moreover, the integration of SEL into daily lesson plans helps students understand how to behave with their peers. Most importantly, however, the students begin to realize that their emotional intelligence is just as important as their academic success.

Instead of specifically doing a lesson on social skills or emotions, try to incorporate these lessons into what you are already teaching. For example, if you're thinking about molecules in science, you might also ask students what form good partnerships.

Another option might be to read a book or talk about a history lesson about a socially challenging situation. Engage the students in a conversation about how to tackle social issues. The lesson then becomes about literacy, history, and emotional and social learning.

Engage them

Either helping to solve a difficult math problem or creating a set of class rules at the beginning of the year, involving children in problem-solving of all kinds. For example, if children have trouble waiting for their turn in class, ask students, "Can you think of a way to help you remember to wait for your turn?" You could also get feedback from older students about bullying at school and what they think the school should do to deal with it. The students themselves also come up with the best ideas for tackling issues. Group projects are a useful way for students to learn how to work together, a skill they will need in different areas of life.

Teach them determination and perseverance

Self-motivation is a major component of social and emotional learning and a need for children to get things done in life.

Although there are many students who will naturally strive to improve themselves in some way, there are other students in this area who need a little more coaching.

Remind students that they must put forth effort and perseverance to experience success. And if you see them making a really hard effort but still falling short of grade, then praise them for their hard work and encourage them to keep trying until they master it.

Each student should be encouraged to set certain goals so they can feel a sense of achievement. This helps offset negative thoughts and encourages children to dig deep and find the will to succeed.

Design and instill respect

It's an important life lesson to remember to be respectful towards others. Clearly, the respectful use of language and motivating children to imitate your actions are one of the best ways of modeling respect. You can also model respect by being mindful and valuing the cultural backgrounds of children and the language.

Encourage the students to do likewise

They should learn to respect one another even if they vary or disagree. Remind them they don't have to agree with someone to treat them respectfully. Note, it also avoids bullying by instilling empathy and is a vital part of education.

Incorporate education on the character

Character education encourages students to develop ethically and responsibly. Teach your students how important it is to have good values, to be honest, to be positive, and to take responsibility for their actions. Give your students opportunities in the classroom to build and fine-tune these skills. Discuss these skills over the course of history lessons and reading activities.

Engage children in learning about ways to become more accountable or trustworthy in the classroom. Let them then put those ideas into practice. Be sure to recognize ethical and honest conduct, especially when students are taking responsibility for negative actions. This does not mean that they should escape discipline, but simply that they recognize the value of being honest.

Encourage the students to build views

Teachers should look for the opinions of their students, allow them to initiate activities, and be flexible when responding to their ideas. Doing so builds the students a sense of competency and increases their desire to learn. You are also less likely to fight envy and jealousy. Envy is often the root cause of bullying, particularly when it comes to relational aggression and mean actions by girls.

Teach them resilience

Research shows more academically successful students being more resilient. They also bounce back faster, they are aware of their opinions, and they understand their beliefs, which gives them a sense of who they are. When bullied, resilient children are less likely to suffer as many consequences as children who are not resilient (Gordon, 2019).

Chapter 6: Using Emotions in Building Relationships

A successful relationship is a result of establishing and maintaining a continuous, healthy link with others. Those who reap the successes of life, happiness, love, and contentment manage to maintain healthy personal and professional relationships with others. They are those of us who are only good at the beginning but find it challenging to keep the relationship intact and improved. The connection eventually fails and falters.

People should know how to nourish the bond or connection in building a relationship, like how to take care of a weak plant. The lack of emotional intelligence is one of the main reasons for a breakdown in relations.

Comprehending Emotional Intelligence

How in a relationship do we perceive emotional intelligence? This is an ability or skill of individuals to successfully understand, control, and express their emotions as well as identify other people's feelings. Having excellent emotional intelligence skills can improve an individual's emotional awareness and a strong emotional base that helps to build good relations.

Possessing the capacity of emotional intelligence in relationships ensures a longer-lasting bond with individuals close to you or those with whom you interact. This should be learned and applied concurrently, however.

It's pointless to know without trying to change or alter the way the relationship is being handled. If you want to achieve successful relationships with those around you, the necessary skills in developing emotional intelligence are presented below. But the essential thing to do is to connect with the core of your emotions before you can pass on your feelings properly and also understand the feelings of other people.

The ability to exhibit emotional intelligence requires five essential skills that should be applied by each individual to build and maintain healthy relations —

First, the ability to manage tension. While stress is natural, it does weaken your emotions and disrupts rational thinking.

Above all, tension is rife at work. Weak or broken lines of communication with colleagues lead to poor relation-building. Identifying when stress levels start to get out of hand and managing stress situations before it damages the relationship becomes imperative.

The second qualification is the ability to recognize and manage our emotions. Our feelings are influenced by our life experiences and everyday interactions with people and situations. We need to be on guard with our emotions in order to communicate well with the people we are dealing with, learn to recognize them, and know-how these feelings affect our relationships with others. In addition to having good communication, emotional awareness helps us understand our needs and motivations.

The ability to communicate nonverbally is the third significant skill we need to learn and improve. That type of communication is stronger than mere words. Our body language transmits thoughts and messages, so this ability is highly visual. Communicate properly to maintain a strong partnership by careful use of facial expressions, gestures, eye contact, body movements, and our language.

The fourth skill in the relationship is the ability to use humor and to play. Good humor in a relationship lifts a distressing situation and gives us a sense of relief from a challenging experience. Individuals should work out certain discrepancies through humor and playfulness, taking the relationship issues lightly.

The final skill in the relationship is the ability to resolve conflicts. Our personal and professional affiliations with people don't always run smoothly. Demonstrate emotional intelligence during disputes by responding appropriately to and addressing any dispute or disagreement with others. Understand the inevitability but manageability of conflicts. And when appropriate emotional intelligence is implemented in dealing with it, conflicts would prove productive and helpful in stabilizing relationships with the work. Manifesting proper emotional intelligence in relationship building brings many advantageous outcomes for the individuals and the connection they create. Professional relationships are strengthened because the colleagues have an understanding and open communication.

This makes it easy for members of the team to iron out any workplace failures and even mend wounded feelings. Good and healthy working relationships create a happy and healthy work environment so individuals can work with each other more comfortably (Exforsys, 2010).

6.1 Ways to Improve Your Relationships

Many important reasons to improve the EQ would make you better at, well, essentially all.

1. It makes you more open to change

One constant in most partnerships is changing: you're likely to change jobs, houses, and personality ticks— not to mention hairstyles— through a long-term relationship. Fortunately, for emotionally intelligent individuals who can imagine and understand these changes in both themselves and their partners, it's easier to adopt these new developments in your relationship, rather than running away from them.

2. It can help you anticipate the needs of your partner

Knowing what your partner requires before they even ask can serve you well in a relationship, whether you give them ash The Bonne News? People with emotional intelligence are especially adept at this skill.

"EQ helps you predict the needs of your loved one, and wants to be more precise," says Dr. Inna Khazan, Ph.D. "You'll be more likely to get the right gift or say the right thing to console them when they're having a hard time.

3. It helps you accept criticism

For a partnership to stay healthy, both partners need to develop together, which often includes both knowing what your partner really likes about you and what they think you might be able to work on.

4. It helps you reflect on your interests

With work and other obligations impacting your relationships, and it's easy to lose sight of your partner's life, you're happy to have. Nonetheless, for those with practiced emotional intelligence, knowing what you value in your relationship and taking time out to prioritize, your partner can feel like a healthy — and easy — choice.

5. It improves your emotional flexibility

If you wish to be the kind of partner your significant other still feel like they can tell anything to, it's time to start working on your emotional intelligence now. Being emotionally intelligent means that you are attuned to both your and your partner's emotional needs, making it simple for them to come to you when they need guidance or support.

6. It helps you roll with the punches

Every relationship has its tough times, and in many cases, it is impossible to see them coming. But, for those with high levels of emotional intelligence, they realize that making things work with someone they love is well worth weathering ups and downs instead of running away when the going gets hard.

7. It helps you see the good in others

After a long time together, and it's pretty easy to start taking someone for granted. However, if you're particularly emotionally smart, it's easier to recognize when you don't appreciate your partner as much as you could and correct your behavior to remedy that mistake. EQ also lets you understand whether your companion behaved in error accidentally or took you for granted, rather than thinking they're doing it some way to upset you. For vague experiences, EQ lets you give your loved ones the benefit of the doubt. You might have asked your partner to bring your favorite kind of tea to the grocery store, for example. He or she returns with another kind of tea. It may be easy to assume that it wasn't enough for your spouse to get the right thing and then tell them how it hurts your feelings and then gets into an argument about it. Being able to give your partner the benefit of the doubt might lead you to think that your favorite kind of tea may have been out of the shop, but he/she has done their best to get you something that you'll like almost as much.

8. It helps you stay committed

While even the healthiest marriages wax and wane, all long-term partnerships have one thing in common: people who remain committed to them. If you're emotionally intelligent, understanding how devastating your significant other's loss of fidelity or partnership would be can help you stay emotionally invested in the long run. Since one study reveals that emotional intelligence accounted for more than 40 percent of total marital satisfaction among couples studied.

9. It may help you get the things you ask for

Roommates, emotional intelligence is also of surprising importance. While many roommates are at odds as they believe that the people with whom they stay can predict their needs, emotional intelligence will make you a better communicator, making it easier to make your needs known and to fulfill them.

"EQ helps you ask with a higher likelihood of success what you need," Dr. Khazan says. "Let's imagine that your roommate was very loud early in the morning, slamming doors and running around, waking up and disrupting your sleep. You yell at them, tell them to stop, and let you sleep. It's unlikely to make your roommate quieter. Or you could say something like:' I know you've had to wake up earlier lately, and it's hard to get up so early!

10. It makes it easier to compromise

The key to getting along with your roommate. Luckily, it is not such a big deal for those with high emotional intelligence quotients to come to a compromise, whether it's about whose job it's to empty the dishwasher or where to place the sofa in the living room. It is easy for emotionally intelligent people to understand the viewpoint of your roommate and balance it carefully against yours, instead of simply assuming you're right.

11. It will make you less codependent

Codependency is very common and can have a negative effect over time on even the tightest roommate pairs. If you are looking to reduce issues with codependency in your relationship with your roommate, start by working on your emotional intelligence. You will loosen your grip as you know the strain that extreme codependency will take on your relationship. Better yet, emotional intelligence makes contentment easier to find, even if you are alone.

12. It reduces passive-aggressive behavior

You can quickly put a damper on any relationship with your roommate. Emotionally intelligent people do not resort to being passive-aggressive in order to get their point across; they simply say that they let other people know what they need and value the needs of others, in return.

13. It helps you resolve conflict more comfortably

Of course, even the closet roommates get into conflicts sometimes. However, the good news for those with adequate emotional intelligence is that prioritizing effective, kind conflict resolution trumps winning an argument, and that, in turn, helps keep things civilian and maintains a long-term relationship.

14. It Makes You More Patient

For parents, emotional intelligence can have profound impacts on their patients. While parents with a low EQ often subconsciously prioritize their needs over their children's ones, the opposite approach is taken by emotionally intelligent parents. Instead of assuming that their children have adult skills or abilities, emotionally smart parents realize that their children do things differently, and sometimes in ways that can be disappointing, and understand that that's all right.

15. It helps you meditate sibling rivalry

Sibling rivalry is a natural part of a sibling, but thankfully, parents who are emotionally intelligent have the skills to mediate it. It's easy to help your k by knowing when it's necessary to step in when it's a good idea to let your children figure things out on their own, and how to be impartial while addressing their problems with them (CROW, 2018).

Chapter 7: Improving Your Social Skills to Become Successful

In emotional intelligence, the term' social skills' refers to the abilities required to effectively control and manipulate the emotions of other people. This may sound like manipulation, but in fact, it can be as easy as knowing that smiling at people makes them smile back and thus can make them feel much more optimistic.

Therefore social skills can be considered the final component of the' jigsaw' emotional intelligence.

7.1 Social Skills

Social skills are the abilities that we use to communicate and engage with each other, both verbally and nonverbally, through movements, body language, and our personal appearance.

People are sociable creatures, and we have evolved many ways to communicate with others about our messages, thoughts, and feelings.

What is said is affected by both verbal language and how we use it-voice tone, speech speed, and the words we use as well as more subtle signals such as body language, gestures, and other non-verbal methods of communication?

The idea that some people are stronger' social interactors' than others has contributed to detailed research into the essence and role of interpersonal interaction.

The development of social skills is about learning how we communicate with others, the messages we send, and how communication strategies can be enhanced to make the way we communicate more productive and successful.

Social Skills attributes. Social skills are goal-driven.

Socially skilled behaviors are interrelated in the sense that at the same time, for the same reason, one person can use more than one type of behavior.

The social skills should be sufficient for the contact situation. For professional and personal contact, various social skills will be used.

Social skills can be defined as certain types of behavior by which a person can be judged on how well they are socially skilled.

You can teach, practice, and learn social skills.

Social skills should be under the individual's cognitive control-learning them involves learning when to use specific behaviors, what behaviors to use, or how to use them.

You can use social skills apps to learn more about what the word 'Social Skills' means.

In this way, the appreciation of social skills leads us to believe that social skills can be acquired, typically through practice and experience, but also taught.

7.2 Improving Your Social Skills Using Emotional Intelligence

Once you can understand and control yourself, then you start to understand other people's emotions and feelings (empathy) and eventually affect them (social skills).

The word 'social skills' covers a wide range of competencies.

In the sense of emotional intelligence, social skills include:

- Persuasion and power skills
- Communication skills
- Conflict management skills
- Leadership skills

- Changing management skill
- Building bonds
- Teamwork and cooperation Team-working skills.

Persuasion and Influence:

Building Charisma how often do you need to convince others to do something?

It's a circumstance that happens almost every day, whether it's getting your teen to tidy up their room, or your preschooler to get ready, or a colleague to attend a meeting on your behalf. Many people seem to be able to do this easily and almost without acknowledging anybody, while others fall back on their position's power to enforce what they want.

Like any other, persuasive skills can be learned, and they are a major part of being able to influence others to reach your goals and ambitions.

Ways to Control and Convince

We all know people who are actively trying to persuade by conversation. They seem to believe they can ground others to exhaustion simply by endlessly reiterating their point of view. Yet, as a general rule, others have still not bought into the idea in this way, and are not committed to it. This means the idea could easily just weaken and die when the going gets tough.

Coercion some fall back on their position's strength and order someone to do whatever they want. This is bullying in its unpleasant sense. Once again, they won't necessarily like what their families or colleagues are doing. If it is difficult, they might well give up. Again it may be futile, as those involved do it because they have to, not because they want to.

A Better Way Then the' Holy Grail' of persuasion is to get others to buy into the idea and will do it that way. And the best way to do that is in a way other people don't notice. But how do you?

The sun and wind fable is a good example: The wind and the sun decided to have a competition to decide who is great once and for all. They agreed the winner would be the one who would be able to convince a man to take off his coat. The wind blew and swept, but the man held his coat just tighter. Then the sun shone gently down, and the man pulled off his coat within minutes.

The moral here is that you cannot force anyone to do what they don't want; rather, the power of persuasion is to get them to desire what you want. Good Persuasion Research shows there are a number of things about good persuaders that people appreciate.

Work by Kurt Mortensen shows that these components are in a large emotional measure. These include keeping promises, being trustworthy and assuming responsibility, being sincere, truthful and honest, understanding their topic and believing in it, building relationships, and being entertaining, as well as not arguing and offering workable solutions.

Therefore, the key skills for effective persuasion are quite broad. First of all, positive persuaders tend to be more generally high in self-esteem and strong Emotional Intelligence. We really do believe they're going to succeed.

Therefore, you have to consider how the audience thinks.

Empathy and good listening skills, like active listening, are key skills here. Normally, if you listen, the audience will tell you what they think and how they think. It also helps to build relationships; people like the ones that take time to become a partner, as well as an influencer. It really follows: if we are truthful, we would all rather do what a friend recommends than someone we hate, however sensible the idea may be. Building a relationship also helps build faith. Effective persuasions or influencers have very good communication skills as well.

It's important you can quickly and efficiently get your point across. Otherwise, you'll never persuade anyone of the merits of your argument.

It is arranging the final skills of successful persuaders. They do their homework, know their audience, and know their subject matter. They took the time to plan themselves and talk about what they want to achieve.

Communication skills

Communication skills are essential for good emotional intelligence. You need to be able to listen to others, and to express your own opinions as well as emotions, perhaps more importantly.

Perhaps the most crucial of all life-skills is being able to communicate effectively. It is what helps us to pass on knowledge to others and to consider what is being said to us. You just have to watch a baby listening to his mother attentively and trying to repeat the sounds she makes to understand how important the need to communicate is.

In its easiest form, communication is the act of transferring information from one location to another. It can be oral (using voice), written (using printed or digital media such as books, newspapers, blogs or emails), visual (using icons, maps, charts or graphs) or non-verbal (using body language, gestures, and the sound and pitch of voice). For action, several of these are often a mixture.

Communication skills can take a lifetime to master — if anybody can claim to have mastered them ever. However, there are a lot of things you can do fairly easily to develop your communication skills and ensure you are able to effectively transmit and receive information.

Importance of good communication skills

The improvement of your communication skills will benefit any aspect of your life, from your work life to social life and everything in between.

The capability to accurately, simply and as intended, convey knowledge is a vital life skill and something that should not be ignored. Building on your communication skills is never too late, and by doing so, you may well find that you are enhancing your quality of life.

Communication skills are needed in almost every aspect of life: Professionally, if you are applying for jobs or pursuing advancement with your current employer, you will almost definitely need to show good communication skills.

Communication skills are needed to properly speak with a wide variety of people while maintaining good eye contact, display a varied vocabulary and tailor your language to your audience, listen effectively, present your ideas properly, write clearly and concisely, and work well in a group. Many of these are essential skills which most employers are looking for.

Verbal communication skills rank first among the' must-have' abilities and attributes of a job candidate. According to the National Association (NACE) survey 2018. When your career progresses, the value of communication skills increases; it's important for most managers and leaders to be able to speak, listen, query, and write with consistency and conciseness.

Good communication skills will strengthen your personal relationships in your personal life by helping you understand and appreciate others.

It's almost a cliché that contact is required in personal relationships. Failure to talk has been pointed for the collapse of any number of friendships and relationships but also an important element is the ability to listen.

It is also important in widening family relationships, whether you want to negotiate holiday plans or make sure your teenage kids are well and happy. Communication skills also ensure that you are capable of managing interactions with businesses and organizations. Over the course of your life, you are likely to have to communicate with a wide range of organizations and institutions. Good communication skills will improve these encounters and ensure that you can get your point across respectfully and simply, as well as take the responses into consideration.

One important skill is being able to complain politely, for example, as is taking criticism yourself. Good communication skills will improve the way you move in life, smoothing your path with others in your relationships.

Poor communication skills will make business-to-person relationships unpleasant and make your life much harder.

Apparently, some people understand how to communicate without even trying. We can adapt their vocabulary, sound, and message to their audience and easily and succinctly get their point in a way that is understood. They are also able to quickly pick up the messages sent to them, knowing both what is being said and what was not being said.

Along the way, they have also developed a good understanding of themselves (called self-awareness) and the patterns of focusing on success and failure, and the behaviors that have led to one or the other.

Interpersonal communication skills

Interpersonal skills are the abilities that we use when we participate in face-to-face contact with one or more other people.

What is communication? And social concepts

We will help you understand the basics and begin to be conscious of what you might need to change.

Improving communication provides information on how you can start tackling these issues. In particular, there may be issues related to intercultural communication, especially if you work or frequently communicate with people from other cultures.

Verbal Communication

Verbal communication is about what we are doing, which is an effective way to convey our meaning.

Verbal communication can be written as well as spoken. The terms we choose can make a big difference when it comes to whether people understand us. Consider contacting a young child, for example, or someone who does not speak our own language very well. Under these conditions, you need to use plain language, short sentences, and regularly check your understanding. It's quite different from a chat with an old friend you've known for years, and you might not even have to finish your sentences with it. Similarly, a conversation with a friend is very different from a business meeting, and when talking to a client, the words you use might be considerably more technical.

Non-verbal Communication,

It involves non-verbal signs, expressions, and expressions of the face, the language of the body, voice tone, and even our appearance. These can either strengthen or contradict our spoken words' meaning, so careful consideration is important. Listening is also a critical interpersonal communication ability.

Communication is a two-way mechanism, as we have said above.

Listening is an essential part of the information we receive. We spend 45 percent of our time listening as we talk. Many people take listening as a matter of course, but it's not the same as hearing and should be considered an ability.

Using communication skills

Good communication skills can also help you provide feedback efficiently, and in a way that does not cause offense: a life-long critical skill.

Strong interpersonal communication skills help us to work in groups and teams more efficiently, which can be formal or informal. Other communication skills include skills, even in a wide range of circumstances, far more than mere verbal and nonverbal contact. The skills we use to maintain a healthy body and mind are personal skills. Yet they, too, will improve communication.

For example, increasing your self-esteem and developing your confidence will help you feel more optimistic about yourself and your ability to communicate. And the first step to act more positively, and therefore effectively, is to feel positive.

You are more likely to be charismatic by having a better understanding of yourself and a more comfortable and optimistic outlook on life, a trait that can further assist the communication process.

Conflict management skills

Conflicts and contradictions may occur at any time, often arising out of thin air.

The practice of conflict management and resolution is important at home and in the workplace. This starts by recognizing the importance of strategy and diplomacy and how it can be used to help diffuse difficult situations.

Good conflict managers are able to open up and settle conflicts. We use emotion sharing to facilitate dialogue and open discussion, minimize the secret currents and issues, and help each group understand the emotions of each other as well as their rational position. We also try to obtain win-win outcomes. Interpersonal conflict is a natural part of life and can occur in almost any field, from organizations through to personal relationships. It is, therefore, necessary for everyone to know how to solve it efficiently, in a way that does not raise the stress levels. Those with strong conflict resolution skills generally help organizations and associations to work more effectively.

Interpersonal conflict is defined as a conflict among two or more individuals.

Chambers English Dictionary describes conflict as "a violent collision: a fight or contest: a battle: a mental struggle."

Personal and social conflict can, therefore, come up with a different disagreement. To become 'conflict,' however, those concerned will intensify it beyond the dispute to something more.

In a workplace, interpersonal conflict is defined as what occurs when an individual or group of people attempt to prevent another person or group from reaching their goals.

Types of Interpersonal Conflict

The first step to resolving conflicts is to determine which technique to use to resolve them. However, you need to identify the root source of the conflict, and hence its type, before you can do that.

There are three types of conflicts,

- Personal or relational conflicts,
- Strategic conflicts, and
- Conflicts of interest:

Personal or relational conflicts are typically about identity or self-image, or important aspects of a relationship such as commitment, breach of trust, perceived deception, or disrespect.

Instrumental conflicts are about objectives, frameworks, processes, and means: something relatively concrete and formal for a person or within the organization.

Conflicts of interest related to how the means of achieving goals, such as time, energy, space, and workers, are allocated. These may also be linked to such variables as relative importance, or knowledge and expertise. One example would be a couple who disagree about whether to spend a bonus on holiday or fix the roof.

Leadership Skills as part of social skills can sound strange

Emotional intelligence is definitely part of leadership, not the other way around?

The response is that emotional intelligence and leadership skills are inextricably linked. As we noted earlier, only those who are attuned to the feelings of themselves and others can expect to affect them. Perhaps power is the key aspect of good leadership, and being able to take others along with you. Some people call that charm, but it's simpler than that: its good emotional intelligence. There's a common debate about what makes a good leader — in other words, what leadership skills are. It is clear that the capability to lead effectively depends on a number of key skills, but also that there are very different characteristics and styles in different leaders.

In fact, there is no right way to lead in all circumstances, and one of the main features of good leaders is their versatility and adaptability to changing circumstances. Employers are very much looking for leadership skills as they include communicating with people in a way that motivates, enthuses, and creates respect.

Whether or not leadership itself can be taught, there's no doubt that the best leaders have a number of core skills. Like any other, those skills can be learned.

Good leaders will be able to articulate a vision and enthuse others with it, not being in a formal leadership role to provide guidance, promoting and directing colleagues' success while holding them accountable, and leading by example.

1. Strategic thinking skills

Maybe the most important skill a leader needs — and what really sets leaders apart from managers — is being able to think strategically.

It means having an idea or dream of where you want to be and working to achieve it, in simple terms.

The good strategic planners see the big picture and are not disturbed by small or side problems. All their decisions will likely be loosely focused on their answer to the question,' does this get me close to where I desire to be? Of course, being able to create a compelling vision, they should also be able to convey it to their followers, which is partly why communication skills are important for leaders as well effectively.

Dream formation is not just a matter of having an idea. A good strategic analysis must be based on evidence, which ensures that information can be gathered and analyzed from a wide variety of sources. It's not just about numbers; it's about knowing and understanding the business and clients, and then -and this is critical-using that information to support your strategic decisions.

2. Planning and Execution Skills

While it is important to be personally organized and empowered as a leader.

Those fields are key management capabilities, but these will also be able to be turned to by the best leaders. Without the plan to go back it into reality, the world's best dream is no good.

Therefore, preparation and action planning go alongside strategic thinking, both necessary for achieving your vision and strategy. Project management and project planning also provide useful skills for administrators and leaders alike. Effective risk management is also essential to help prevent things from going wrong and to handle them when they do.

Good leaders, too, often have very powerful facilitation skills to effectively manage groups.

Leaders also need to be capable to make perfect decisions to help the execution of their agenda and to solve problems. Problems can become resources and learning experiences with a positive attitude, and a leader can gain a lot of insight from a problem discussed.

3. Skills of managing people

There are no leaders without followers. Therefore, leaders need expertise in dealing with others on a one-to-one and group basis, and a variety of techniques in their armor to manage a wide range of situations. Many of these skills are important to managers too, In particular, leaders are supposed to inspire and empower their followers by developing a motivating atmosphere, both explicitly.

One of the first qualities to be learned by new leaders is how to delegate. For many people, this is a difficult skill, but, well done, the delegation will give accountability to team members and a taste to leadership itself and help them stay motivated Delegating work within a team is further difficult, including juggling workloads, and ensuring that resources are given to everyone to help them develop.

Both members and managers need to consider how a team can be built and controlled. We need to learn how to recruit efficiently and use recruitment procedures to bring people' on board.' You also need to understand the importance of controlling efficiency, both on a regular basis and managing bad performance.

4. Management of Change and Development Skills

Change may seem like a peculiar companion to people managing and talking, but leadership is often particularly important in times of change.

To lead an organization through the process, a leader needs to understand change management. For example, change management involves an impelling vision to be developed and shared. It also involves strongly pushing the transition forward, and leadership to make it' stick' if the company is not to revert within a very short period of time.

Chapter 8: stop overthinking

What went wrong? You forgot the date of birth of your best friend. What's up in your mind? Did she get hurt? Is she all angry at me? Does she ever speak to me again? Is she going to celebrate my birthday? Will she decide not to give me a birthday? Can she say every one of our friends? Does she hate me? If you are, then you're a classic over-thinker! And it's cool to think about things, but over-thinking isn't! This is a problem, and there are ways to overcome this problem.

8.1 What is Overthinking?

Instead of behaving and doing stuff, when you worry too much, you overthink. Instead of behaving, you overthink while you evaluate, complain, and echo the same thoughts over and over again.

This habit prevents you from acting. It wastes your resources, disables your decision-making ability, and keeps putting you on a loop of thought and dreaming.

This is sort of thought that is wasting your time and resources and stopping you from doing new activities and making progress in your life.

It is like tying yourself to a cord that is attached to a pole and going back and forth in circles.

There's more possibility of stress, anxiety, and lack of inner peace in this situation.

On the other hand, you become more effective, more relaxed, and happier when you don't overthink.

8.2 Disadvantages of Overthinking

Never get done over-thinking yes, you may deny it, but you know it's true. It's a dangerous trap to ponder about! The deeper you come in, the more you wonder. Really the over-thinking never ends! It continues and continues, making you miss important moments in life.

1. No Actual Action Taken

Over-thinking never ends. You never get to a final decision as a result. And no action is ever taken without a final decision. All it thinks and all it does. You are only thinking about something deeply that doesn't result in it becoming a reality. If something has to be achieved, to do it, one has to move their hands and legs. So just stop thinking and do it!

2. Complicates Things

When you over-think something, you are probably making it more difficult. In your mind, over-thinking turns something simple into something so complicated, to the point where it seems difficult to get out of the complication. Earlier, a little effort would fix all problems for you, but now every step you take will most definitely seem like a step on a bed of thorns.

3. Living in Fear

As you just over-think and never take action, you never know what the outcome is going to be; and this terrifies you. An over-thinker goes on looking at every circumstance and possibility of the worst possible outcomes. It cripples your inner strength and paralyzes you with fear. Lack of Confidence

An over-thinker assumes that everything around them will go wrong. More often, they're pessimists than not. Over-thinking and its resultant pessimism place you in a situation in which you have no respect for yourself.

You don't trust your own capabilities and are always alert to possible whispers of your incompetence.

4. Depression

You've thought so much of all the bad things that can happen to you that you're living in constant anxiety that those thoughts will become real. A drop of a hat can fill you with fear and despair. The way you think, too, is the way that you feel. Constant negative thoughts will constantly leave you feeling negative. In the end, this could turn into depression.

5. This increases your chances of developing mental illness.

A study published in the Journal in 2013, which focuses on your failures, errors, and problems, increases your risk of mental health issues.

And rumination can make you up for a vicious, hard to break the loop. Ruminating causes havoc to your mental health. When your mental health decreases, so do your ability to ruminate.

6. Issue-solving interferes.

Research shows over thinkers feel that by rehashing their issues in their minds, they are supporting themselves. Nevertheless, studies show a paralysis of the analysis is possible.

Anything overanalyzing interferes with problem-solving. It can cause you to dwell on the problem, instead of seeking solutions.

Even easy decisions, like choosing what to wear for an interview or deciding where to go on vacation. When you're overthinking, it can feel like a life-or-death decision. Ironically, this whole idea won't help you make a better choice.

7. It upsets your sleep.

If you're an over-thinker, you probably already know that you can't sleep because your mind is not going to shut off.

Studies confirm this, showing that ruminants and anxiety lead to fewer sleeping hours. Until you drift off, you will be more likely to toss and turn for hours.

But later sleeping may not help as overthinking also impairs your sleep quality. You'll be less prone to falling into a deep sleep after worrying about the same thing again and again.

8.3 Signs of Overthinking

Planning your decisions carefully is a vital aspect of making good choices, but we were all in those circumstances where we ended up focusing on it longer than we should have been. Watching for signs that you overthink things too much is helpful because all that ruminating could end up holding you back. Some thoughts are needed, but other times you may find yourself reading too much into a situation too unnecessarily or wasting too long making a decision when it's easier to just go with your instinct. It's always necessary to weigh your options and make wise choices, but you don't want your thoughts to end up harming you. When you like you're wasting too much time worrying about every aspect of your life, look out for these signs that you're overthinking things too much to really affect you.

1. You ignore your instincts

If you tend to ignore your intestinal instincts and make long lists of pros and cons.

You probably overthink it, "says Odes sky. "Your intuition is a surprisingly accurate tool: research published in the journal Proceedings of the National Academy of Sciences found that when study participants were forced to choose between two instinct-only options, they made the correct call up to 90 percent of the study. Thinking about it, you are wasting your emotional energy and can leave you feeling physically and emotionally drained.

2. "When it seems more convenient to stop conversations with others or actually find solutions instead of replaying things in your head, this encourages overthinking and can lead you to talk out of something," says psychologist Marni Amsellem, Ph.D. via email. You'll need to face the dispute head-on.

3. You Miss Deadlines

You're likely overthinking decisions if the deadline you've given yourself has come and gone, many times. "You want to delay, even after you have set yourself a deadline," Odes sky says.

4. You Repeat the Same Conversations to Your Friends

When you overthink something, you always run it over with your friends, and it might be too much if they start getting irritated. "Your friends get tired of being asked again and again about the same thing," Odessky says. "Or perhaps you're embarrassed to bring it up because they've seen it a million times earlier."

5. You Need Every Piece of Information to Make Up Your Mind

Some information is needed in making a decision, but somewhere you have to draw the line. "To overthink something too much means you're not going to be satisfied until you've read everything on the subject and asked suggestions from everyone until you make up your mind," says Ode's sky.

6. You're not emotionally present around others

Overthinking stuff will cause you to spend a lot of time in your head, which means you're not completely emotionally present when you're around others. "If you concentrate on your thoughts rather than the person before you, it can make them feel you're not interested in them or what they're telling you, which can, of course, be harmful to the relationship," Allen says. Try to ground yourself by really focusing on where you are in the moment.

7. "Your overthinking keeps you off

When fear stops you from doing anything or going ahead in your life," says Allen. "It usually involves" what if? "Thoughts, and then thoughts about all the stuff that might go wrong."

8.4 Ways to Stop Overthinking

How to stop overthinking

It's easier said than done to put an end to rehashing, second-guessing, and disastrous predictions. But you can limit your negative thinking habits by doing consistent practice:

1. Note if you think too much

Perception is the first step to avoiding overthinking. Start paying attention to your own way of thinking. Recognize that your thoughts aren't constructive when you find yourself replaying events in your mind over and over, or worrying about things you cannot manage.

2. Challenge your thoughts

Negative thoughts can quickly get carried away. Before you conclude that calling in sick will get you fired, or that missing one deadline will leave you homeless, accept that your feelings may be overly negative.

Learn to recognize and remove the errors of thinking until they drive you into complete hysteria.

3. Holding the emphasis on the constructive problem-solving

Dwelling is not helpful in your problems, but searching for solutions is. Tell yourself what steps you should take to learn from an error or prevent a problem in the future. Instead of telling yourself why something happened, wonder what you can do about it.

4. Schedule Time

Thinking about how you might do things in a different way or, for example, understanding potential pitfalls on a plan will help you do better in the future. Incorporate "thinking time" 20 minutes into your daily schedule. Let yourself stress, ruminate, or ponder over whatever you want during this time. Then move on towards something more successful when the time is up. When you find that you overthink things outside of your scheduled time, remember to think about it later.

5. Practice mindfulness

When you are living in the now, it is difficult to rehash yesterday or worry about tomorrow. Make a commitment to become more mindful of the here and now. Mindfulness, like any other skill, takes practice, but over time it can minimize overthinking.

6. Change

The Channel is telling yourself that you should stop thinking about something that might backfire. The more you try to prevent the thought from entering your brain, the more likely it will be to continue to pop up.

The best way to change a channel is to occupy yourself with an operation.

Exercise, engage in conversation on a completely different topic or get involved in a project that distracts your mind from a flood of negative thinking (WOLFF, 2017).

Chapter 9: Using Your Emotions for Personal Growth

9.1 Become master of your emotions

How Emotions Are Made. Unlike the classical theory that emotions are built-in environmentally induced responses, Barrett believes emotions don't happen to us without our will. Instead, we build our emotions by making sense of sensations and making predictions using our past experiences and our concept collection. Therefore, as "architects of our experiences," we don't need to be at the mercy of our emotions— rather, we can learn to master them. Here are seven suggestions to help you do just that:

1. Keep your body in good shape with the budget.

Mastering your emotions starts with maintaining a balanced budget for the body. It is the advice we've all heard before— eating healthily, exercising regularly, getting enough sleep— but science is consistent about it being a prerequisite for a healthy emotional life. At this moment, the simplest way to master your emotions is to move your body, Barrett writes. For example, animals get back into balance regularly through movement. A simple walk (in nature) in the subgenual prefrontal cortex can reduce rumination and reduce neural activity, thus improving mental wellbeing. "Moving yourself can change your predictions, and thus your experience."

Besides the basics of nutrition, sleep, and exercise, it is possible to build a healthy budget for the body through many other means. These include massages, yoga, time out in nature, reading.

Literature invites us to engage in the narrative of somebody else, temporarily pulling us out of our own ruminations. Meditation offers an opportunity to practice emotional observation and experience, and then to release them without judgment. Gratitude, positive social contact is also considered exercises that boost the body's budget. Barrett suggests using them all by forming regular lunch dates with a friend and taking turns to treat each other.

2. Cultivate emotional intelligence.

The term "Emotional Intelligence" may evoke various images, but Barrett refers to "getting your brain to build the most useful instance of the most useful concept of emotion in a given situation." This will require you to fine-tune your emotional concepts: instead of piling all affectively similar emotions under one paraglider term (Barrett uses the example of Awesome for good feelings and "Crappy" for bad ones), try to learn the nuanced meanings of various emotions misery comes in many tastes — bitter, enraged, irritated, — just as there are a lot of ways to feel great The ability to distinguish between the fine nuances of different emotions will not only make you an expert in emotions (a "sommelier of emotions," but will also give your brain more options to "predict and categorize your sensations more effectively, and to better tailor your actions to your environment."

3. Take on new concepts.

"Be a gatherer of experiences," writes Barrett (p. 180). New experiences you accumulate by taking trips, reading books, watching films, gaining new perspectives, trying to eat new and different food, studying foreign languages, even learning new words in your own tongue, offer opportunities to build your experience in new ways. How does this whole novelty help you master your emotions? By encouraging your brain to form new concepts and bind old ones in new ways, thereby affecting your future predictions and behaviors. Expanding your vocabulary, for example, can lead to greater emotional health by providing new concepts which, in turn, can not only help you get better equipped to deal with different circumstances but potentially increase your empathy and improve your negotiating skills.

4. Learn to more fine-tune your emotions.

In helping clients reframe situations, therapists are partly "finding the most useful categorization in the service of action," writes Barrett (p. 182). Learning to distinguish feelings with finer granularity may help people better regulate their emotions, as it gives them more information on how to adjust their behavior and how to handle circumstances (Barrett et al., 2001). Research has even shown that people who can easily differentiate between feelings are less likely to resort to binge-drinking or feel overwhelmed by stress. In a study, when people with a fear of spiders used various words of anxiety and fear to label their emotions (i.e., fine-grained categorization), they became less anxious about spiders. In addition, when graders in 5th and 6th grade enriched their vocabulary of words of emotion, they were able to increase

Their academic performance and attitude in school. In contrast, individuals with social anxiety and depressive disorders tend to exhibit and experience less differentiated negative emotions in their daily lives (i.e., categorization with low grains).

5. Take a look at the positive experiences.

Concepts are reinforced and enshrined in our world model if we draw our attention to them. Savoring and attending to optimistic ideas will make them more popular, which in turn will help you to predict and foster potential positivity. One easy way to recall positive experiences is to write down them. On the other hand, ruminating about negative events will make it easier for neural networks in your brain to re-create those concepts in the future. "Any experience you build is an investment, so make wise investments," Barrett writes. "Cultivate the future experiences you wish to build again" (p. 183).

6. Deconstruct your emotions, and recategorize them.

Try to deconstruct a feeling into its mere physical sensations, rather than a filter through which you see the world," Barrett writes (p. 188). Deconstruction of your feelings (e.g., anxiety) down to their physical sensations (e.g., a racing heart) may have surprising advantages. Physical sensations are not personal, to begin with, and are easier to let go of than thoughts and emotions. Also, categorization is useful for behavioral regulation.

For instance, people have demonstrated improved performance in public speaking and testing after categorizing anxiety into the natural way a body copes. Learning to separate physical sensations from the bad feelings that accompany them can even help chronic pain sufferers crave less pain and see pain as a mere physical sensation rather than a "personal disaster" (Barrett, 2012).

The way we interpret our inner states can, in short, affect our emotions and behavior. "When you're feeling bad, treat yourself like you've got a virus, rather than assuming your unpleasant feelings are personal. Your feelings could only be noise," Barrett writes (p. 194).7.

7. Cultivate Awe —

The sentiment that dwells "in the upper reaches of happiness and on the boundary of fear" can boost our body budgets in various ways. Experiencing awe has proved to be a strong predictor of lower levels of proinflammatory cytokines (molecules associated with a number of illnesses at elevated levels). Awe inspires curiosity, interconnection, and a desire for exploration (Stellar et al., 2015). Nature, in particular, offers innumerable opportunities to experience awe. Awe evokes the sweeping presence of vastness from the still of the freshly-fallen snow on a mountain peak of a turbulent sea or a faultless rainbow. We can come back to it again and again as we cultivate awe, showing the gift of a new view, and at times a much-needed distance from ourselves (photos an, 2017).

9.2 Control Your Anger by Using Emotions

Anger is a natural and automatic response to the pain of one form or another emotional or physical. Anger can occur when people feel unwell, feel dismissed, feel threatened, or experience some loss. No matter what type of pain, the important thing is that the pain experienced is unpleasant. Because anger never occurs in solitary confinement but occurs after feelings of pain, it is often characterized as an emotion of second hand.

Pain alone isn't sufficient to cause aggression. Anger happens when pain is combined with some thought which triggers anger. Thoughts that may trigger anger include personal assessments, assumptions, evaluations, or situational interpretations that make people think someone else is (consciously or not) trying to hurt them. Anger is a social emotion in this sense; you always have a goal against which your anger is directed (even if that goal is yourself). Combined with anger-triggering emotions, feelings of pain inspire you to take action, face threats, and protect yourself by hitting yourself against the target that you believe causes you pain. By this, we mean people sometimes become angry, so they don't have to feel pain. People are transforming their feelings of pain into anger because it feels better to be angry than to be in pain. This transformation of pain into anger can happen consciously or unconsciously.

Being angry rather than just in pain has a number of advantages, notably distraction among them. People who are in pain generally think of their pain. Angry people though think of harming those who caused pain. Part of changing pain into anger involves a shift of attention–from focusing on oneself to focusing on others. Anger thus temporarily protects the individual from having to recognize their real painful feelings and deal with them; instead, you get to worry about getting back to the people you are angry with. Becoming angry can help you hide the reality that you find a situation scary or that you feel vulnerable to it.

Becoming angry also creates a sense of righteousness, power, and being better than others when someone is just in pain. You're angry with cause when you're angry. The common refrain is, "The people who hurt me are wrong–they should be punished." It is very unlikely that somebody gets angry with somebody that they don't think hurt them in some significant way.

Defining whether someone's anger is an issue often turns on whether or not other people agree with them that their anger is justified, and the actions they take in the name of their anger. Angry people most often feel justified in their anger.

Others don't always agree with them. Anger's social judgment creates real consequences for the wrathful individual. An angry person may feel justified in carrying out an angry, aggressive action, but if a peer judge or jury does not see it that way, then that angry person may still go to prison. If a supervisor denies that anger towards a customer is justified, then a job may still be lost. If a spouse does not agree that anger was justified, there may be problems with a marriage.

The seductive sense of superiority associated with indignation, whether justified or unjustified, provides a powerful temporary boost to self-esteem. Feeling angry is more satisfying than acknowledging the painful sentiments associated with vulnerability. Use anger to transform sensations of vulnerability and helplessness into feelings of control and power. Some individuals develop an unconscious habit of transforming nearly all their bad feelings into anger so that they can avoid having to deal with it. The question is that even if the frustration distracts you from feeling vulnerable, you still feel vulnerable at some point. Anger can't make the pain go away-it just distracts you from it. Anger doesn't necessarily fix or address the issues that made you feel afraid or vulnerable in the first place, and it can create new problems, including social and health concerns.

Anger is an exceedingly strong emotion. When you continually show it, other people will avoid you like the plague. On the other hand, hold it bottled up in, and you become a pressure cooker that will inevitably blow its top — - leading to actions you regret later on.

Emotional intelligence is extremely helpful in helping you effectively deal with anger. Recognizing that you need to pick your battles will help you to become overly anxious and possibly burn out.

For instance, a situation could cause you to get angry because you don't fully understand it. You may be witnessing an action and perceiving it as an injustice, but each situation has context and background to it, much of which you are not aware of. Having that in mind will keep you from ending up in situations that don't really involve you.

And if some people or situations get your blood to boil (and you don't need it for your daily work), why not just avoid it to the extent possible?

A Balanced View

The truth is when you're right to get angry; there are plenty of instances.

Let's say a certain colleague of yours gets really on your nerves, for example. You know the type— they always leave unwashed dishes in the sink, constantly complaining, often disrespectful. You have endured this behavior for a while, and you are moved to do something about it one day.

There's something positive about your anger: it's time to address an unacceptable situation.

So, how are you progressing? You could just go off on your colleague, call him out publicly on all of his negative behaviors, and tell him everybody's sick and tired of that. Will that change the way he behaved? Probably. But is that really the way you want to deal with the situation? This will not only adversely affect your relationship with this coworker, but it can also damage your reputation.

Conversely, if you take time to think through your actions and their consequences, your strategy will be much more effective. Of course, you're not always going to be inspired to sit back and reflect on the situation in the heat of the moment. That's why learning to keep control is important.

Controlling your anger is like being fired. It may be a useful instrument, or it may be hideously destructive.

Some situations require an immediate response as if you are witnessing some type of abuse or bullying, whether physical or psychological. But in other cases, smaller things might cause your anger to build-up to the point where you risk losing control over your emotions.

If you feel this is joyful to you, then try:

1. Leave the place

If you are in the middle of a situation that is extremely uncomfortable, it's hard not to say the first thing that comes to mind. Get away from the situation before you do or say something that you'll surely regret.

2. Plunge yourself into something you enjoy.

Search for something to indulge in that will distract your attention and help you to calm down until you take a break from the situation. Try reading, listening to music, or any other relaxing activity that you find.

3. Try non-strenuous workouts.

Go for a walk, ride a bike, or stretch yourself. That can relieve muscle tension and help you relax.

From time to time, every one of us will get angry. But using these strategies will help you increase your EQ, control your anger, and express your feelings in a more beneficial way — to you and to others (Matula, 2018).

9.3 Controlling your stress with emotional intelligence

Emotions have the power to override our rational mind. They will affect how we conduct our personal lives, how we run our company, and how we interact with loved ones, friends, clients, employees, etc.

Irrational thinking like this is an obstacle that can only prevent you from progressing and lead to bad relationships, stress, anxiety, and even depression.

Yet working on your EQ will help you get back in charge. For an example of a hobbyist photographer, he brings different lenses that are best suited for the shot he tries to capture. Similarly, getting an increased EQ lets you choose the right view to cope with unpredictable obstacles and troubles that life can throw your way. Based on certain situations, you gain the ability to turn "lenses," so you can look at the world with a different viewpoint for each case, removing emotional baggage that can hinder you from achieving your objectives.

You should understand the two psychological components to boost your EQ: self-awareness and social awareness.

Conclusion

Emotional intelligence is the ability to understand and manage your own emotions as well as understanding other's emotions. Showing empathy to them increasing your social skills you can motivate them to want what you want. Now a day's emotional intelligence is as important as learning AB C. In life if you want to become successful then you must improve your emotional intelligence. it helps in reducing anger and stress and it also makes you able to overcome the problem of overthinking which stops you from taking actions and wastes your time and energy.

References

Ackerman, C. E. (2019). What is Self-Regulation? (+95 Skills and Strategies). pp. **https://positivepsychology.com/self-regulation/**.

Bariso, J. (2018). 13 Signs of High Emotional Intelligence. pp. **https://www.inc.com/justin-bariso/13-things-emotionally-intelligent-people-do.html**.

Beata Souders. (2019). What is Motivation? A Psychologist Explains. pp. **https://positivepsychology.com/what-is-motivation/**.

Cherry, K. (2019). The 3 Key Elements That Makeup Emotion. pp. **https://www.verywellmind.com/what-are-emotions-2795178**.

cmf, B. (2012). How do emotions affect our lives? pp. **http://www.claretianformation.com/how-does-emotions-affect-our-lives/**.

CROW, S. (2018). 30 Ways That Emotional Intelligence Can Make You Better at Everything. pp. **https://bestlifeonline.com/emotional-intelligence-improves-relationships/**.

Exforsys. (2010). Using Emotional Intelligence to Build Relationships. pp. **http://www.exforsys.com/career-center/relationship-management/emotional-intelligence-build-relationships.html**.

Gordon, S. (2019). Strategies for Teaching Children Emotional Intelligence. pp. **https://www.verywellfamily.com/strategies-for-increasing-emotional-intelligence-460606**.

Houston, E. (2020). The Importance of Emotional Intelligence. pp. **https://positivepsychology.com/importance-of-emotional-intelligence/**.

Jessie Zhu, M. M. (2020). What is Self-Awareness and Why is it Important? [+5 Ways to Increase It]. pp. https://positivepsychology.com/self-awareness-matters-how-you-can-be-more-self-aware/.

Matula, G. (2018). How To Use Emotional Intelligence To Deal With Anger. pp. https://www.eqapplied.com/bariso/how-to-use-emotional-intelligence-to-deal-with-anger.

phogosyan, M. (2017). How to Master Your Emotions. pp. https://www.psychologytoday.com/us/blog/between-cultures/201705/how-master-your-emotions.

Pringle, Z. I. (2020). Emotional Intelligence Makes Creativity Happen. pp. https://www.psychologytoday.com/us/blog/creativity-the-art-and-science/202002/emotional-intelligence-makes-creativity-happen.

STOKER, J. (2018). 10 Advantages that Result from Increasing Your Emotional Intelligence. pp. https://www.dialogueworks.com/blog/10-advantages-that-result-from-increasing-your-emotional-intelligence.

TALERNGSRI, A. (2019). The power of emotional intelligence in the digital age. pp. https://www.bangkokpost.com/business/1684232/The-power-of-emotional-intelligence-in-the-digital-age.

What is Empathy? (n.d.). pp. https://greatergood.berkeley.edu/topic/empathy/definition#what-is-empathy.

WOLFF, C. (2017). 10 Signs You Overthink Things Too Much & It's Holding You Back. pp. https://www.bustle.com/p/10-signs-you-overthink-things-too-much-its-holding-you-back-60523.